Essential Manners for Men

What to Do, When to Do It, and Why

Peter Post

HarperResource

An Imprint of HarperCollins*Publishers*

HarperCollins books may be purchased for educational, business, or sales promotional use. For information please write: Special Markets Department, HarperCollins Publishers Inc., 10 East 53rd Street, New York, NY 10022.

FIRST EDITION

Designed by Ralph L. Fowler

Library of Congress Cataloging-in-Publication Data

Post, Peter.
    Essential manners for men : what to do, when to do it, and why / Peter Post.—1st ed.
      p. cm.
    Includes index.
    ISBN 0-06-053980-1
    1. Etiquette for men. I. Title.
  BJ1855.P67 2003
  395.1'42—dc21

2003047885

03   04   05   06   07   WBC/RRD   10   9

For thirty years we have lived together, shared children, owned a business together, gone shopping every week together, renovated one house and built another together. She introduced me to two of the passions of my life: Italy and yoga. She knows and lives by what etiquette is as well as any person I know. Certainly she has corrected me more than a few times, and, as much as I hate to say it, she was almost always right.

Throughout this book she is referred to as "my wife."

But here, it is my pleasure to thank Tricia
for all her help and patience in making this book possible.

CONTENTS

....

Part One: Daily Life

From the middle of the night to the middle of the afternoon, every day brings an unending stream of situations that can make or break your interactions with the people around you. Whether at home, on the street, in the car, on the phone, at the gym, or on the playing field, men face a host of choices which directly affect their relationships with the people around them. On a daily basis, men constantly find themselves in all sorts of situations where they simply aren't sure what to do. Fortunately, the solutions are here.

10 The Sporting Life: On the Field and in the Stands 64

11 Parents and Kids 71

Part Two: Social Life 77

Family, friends, lovers, significant others, prospects—every day we interact with people in all kinds of situations. Whether we're visiting our fiancée's family for the first time or hosting the weekly poker game, life is about dealing with people. How we navigate these waters can make a huge difference in how we're viewed and whether we succeed or fail with others. "Social Life" delves into these situations and sets the stage for smooth sailing.

12 The Top Three Issues in Social Life 79

Part Three: On the Job   141

The office holds its own special set of situations that can stump even the most confident of men. From how to handle your boss's birthday, to dressing for success, to ordering when you're at a business dinner, to the ever-tricky "Do I stand up or not?" question, knowing what to do can make or break the moment—and sometimes your career. Unfortunately, these situations aren't taught in school. Fortunately, we *do* explore them here.

ACKNOWLEDGMENTS

....

I want to offer a very special thank-you to Royce Flippin, who worked tirelessly with me to edit my rambling, run-on writing into a readable text.

Cindy Post Senning and Elizabeth Upham Howell were invaluable as they read every chapter and made sure I stayed on topic. With her expert's knowledge about etiquette, Peggy Post kept my advice on point.

Thank you to Toni Sciarra and Greg Chaput for their understanding, patience, and insightful editing.

Many thanks go to Katherine Cowles, my agent, who believed in this project right from the start and encouraged me to pursue it when I wasn't sure it would ever fly.

Anna Post and Lizzie Post are wonderful daughters who have drawn on their own experiences to help me fine-tune the etiquette advice.

Finally, I want to thank my great-grandmother Emily Post. I have spent a great deal of time reading her original *Etiquette* as well as her novels and other nonfiction books. The more I read and learn about her, the more I realize how truly extraordinary a woman she was. Long before she wrote *Etiquette*, she understood what it meant to be gracious and courteous—or, as she called it, "to have charm." If ever there was a person who had charm, it was she.

And Then the Room
Went Silent

Several months ago, I was sitting at a conference room table in Salt Lake City with a potential client. There were maybe fifteen people around the table—half of them men, half of them women. They all wanted to know a little more about me and about The Emily Post Institute. Among other things, I told them that I had just signed a contract to write a book about men's etiquette.

The room suddenly went silent. Then, just as suddenly, all the women in the room started talking at once—saying, virtually in unison, that when the book was published they wanted to give a copy to every man in their lives.

The men, on the other hand, simply chuckled quietly and rolled their eyes. As they did, I could see their thinking as clearly as if it were stamped across their foreheads: "Read a book about etiquette? *Right!*"

At that moment, I realized something. While women might *buy* the book, in order for it to be successful, men had to *want* to read it.

Once everyone quieted down, I explained to them that what I had in mind was *not* your typical etiquette book. "It's not going to be a reference book," I told them. "Instead, it'll be a book that men can read right through, cover to cover. It's going to be conversational in tone, with plenty of examples to illustrate my points. I'll talk about my *own* failings at etiquette (there have been lots of them, believe me). And most important, I'll explain *why* various manners make sense."

As I've traveled the country, speaking, lecturing, and giving seminars, I've discovered that virtually all men have questions about how to handle various situations in their personal, social, and business lives. I know this because men ask me questions about these situations all the time.

In this book, I've tried to answer these questions in the same way I do in my seminars—by presenting problematic situations that any man is likely to encounter in day-to-day life, and resolving them in an entertaining, engaging, conversational way. Once you've been exposed to the situations in this book and learn how to deal with them *before* they actually happen, you'll have a model to work from when you face similar problems.

This book doesn't strive to be a complete description of every manner, guideline, or etiquette rule in the whole universe. In fact, it only covers about 10 percent of all manners. But this 10 percent represents the cream of the crop. You'll find that the advice I'm offering will apply to 90 percent or more of the situations you'll encounter in your life.

So don't look for advice in these pages on how to address a letter to the President of the United States. You'll have to get that from the big *Emily Post's Etiquette* book. Likewise, you won't learn the difference between a ball and a dance from reading this book, and you certainly won't learn how to fold a dinner napkin. (Just make sure you set one at each place setting.)

What you *will* find is advice that tells you:

> ➤ The areas of a home or apartment where trouble is most likely to occur, and how you can head this trouble off at the pass.

> ➤ The most important behaviors to avoid and those to emulate when you're at a fitness center, in your car, at a wedding, out with friends, at work, in the stands at your kid's baseball game, and many other places men commonly go.

> ➤ The flash points in everyday business life that can derail you, and what you can do to stand out as a rising star.

> ➤ The special things you should do on a date to impress the person you are with.

> ➤ How to be an impeccably thoughtful houseguest—the kind that impresses a special woman's parents to no end, or gets invited back "any time" to your friend's beach house.

As I explained to the group in Salt Lake City, men often have a completely false understanding of what etiquette is and how it can help them in their lives. Many men think etiquette is just for women, or that it's something women "make" men do—so they cringe whenever they hear the word.

In fact, nothing could be further from the truth. Manners and the principles behind manners apply to men just as much as they apply to women. My real goal in this book is to get men to stop cringing at the word "etiquette"—and to help men see how etiquette applies to every aspect of their lives, and how manners can make everything they do easier, smoother, and more successful.

In a nutshell, etiquette really is about treating people with consideration, respect, honesty, and understanding—and manners are the tools that will let you accomplish this with ease, simplicity, and confidence.

—Peter Post
Burlington, Vermont

The "E" Word

Etiquette Is . . .

Good. You've made it this far.

Getting past that "E" word is important. Whenever I give a talk, the first thing I do is ask the audience to define "etiquette." Their response is always the same: "Etiquette is a bunch of rules" . . . "Etiquette is the stuff my mother used to make me do" . . . "Etiquette is the old-fashioned way of doing things."

Meanwhile, they're thinking: "Who needs this stuff?"

Emily Post, my great-grandmother, knew what etiquette really was all about. Sure, she wrote a famous etiquette book, which people imagine is filled with rules. And it's true, there *are* a lot of specific guidelines (Emily called them manners) that dictate how people should act in a given situation. But these guidelines exist for a purpose: to help smooth the way for positive interactions between people by prescribing the ways in which we're expected to act and react to people around us.

When we use the manners that are expected of us, the heavens don't part, and crowds don't applaud us; life just goes on smoothly, the way it should. The importance of manners becomes obvious only when we *don't* use them. For example, one "manner" states that if you say "Hi" or "Good morning" to a person at work, that person should respond in a like manner, since this is the considerate thing to do. So far, so good. But what happens if you said "Hi," and your co-worker didn't say anything in return? How would that make you feel? You'd probably wonder something like, "Did I do something to annoy him?" or, "Doesn't anybody ever notice that I exist?" or even, "Do I smell bad?"

Manners matter. Use them, and you will make the best impression possible.

SURVEY SAYS
When You Behave Well, People Notice

To learn more about how people view men's behavior, we posted four surveys on our Emily Post Institute web site: Daily Life, Social Life, Work Life, and Special Occasions. The results of those surveys helped delineate the topics in this book.

In compiling the survey data, we discovered that the majority of the respondents—86 percent of the total—were women. We also found that their ages varied widely:

➢ 22 percent of the respondents were between 20 and 29

➢ 30 percent were between 30 and 39

➢ 25 percent were between 40 and 49

➢ 23 percent were 50 or over

Most of our respondents were also sharing living quarters with a significant other:

➢ 66 percent of the respondents were married

➢ 7 percent were unmarried but currently living with someone

➢ 16 percent had never been married

For all the variations in age and marital status, one consistent theme emerged in all the surveys: women want men to treat them with respect, and they notice and value men who have good manners. When a man treats others with respect, his image shines in their eyes.

Still, no one can possibly know all the manners there are, or remember precisely how to apply them to every situation. In fact, in today's fast-paced, informal world, manners *don't* always apply in every situation.

Fortunately, the collection of manners that we call etiquette is based on a set of simple but profound principles. Manners and principles are *not* the same thing: manners are specific guidelines that change with time and vary across cultures. For instance, children in the United States are taught to shake hands when meeting someone, while Japanese children are taught to greet people by bowing. While the manners themselves may be different, each is correct for that specific culture, and each exists for the same universal reason: to have a specific way to show respect to people when you greet them.

Etiquette is governed by three principles: consideration, respect, and honesty. These provide the framework for defining every manner that has ever been formulated. Each of these principles is timeless. These principles transcend cultural boundaries, cross socioeconomic boundaries, and apply equally to all ages.

CONSIDERATION is understanding how other people and entities are affected by whatever is taking place. Consideration is empathy. It helps us to assess how a situation affects everyone involved, and then act accordingly.

RESPECT is recognizing that how you interact with another person will affect your relationship with that person, and then choosing to take actions that will build relationships, rather than injure them. Respect helps us decide *how to choose* to act toward others.

HONESTY is being truthful, not deceptive. There is a critical difference, too, between benevolent and brutal honesty: "I have a problem with that," vs. "That's a stupid thing to say." Honesty ensures that we act sincerely.

All of the manners discussed in this book and all the solutions to the situations described in these pages involve the application of these three principles.

"But if etiquette is so simple," you ask, "then why are you writing a whole book on the subject?"

In a word: confidence. When men encounter an unfamiliar situation and are unsure what to do, they often either freeze or make the wrong choice. By reading through the situations and examples in this book, you'll learn how to deal graciously and effectively with a wide variety of problems in daily life, social life, and work life. Even more important, you'll gain the knowledge and confidence to resolve such situations on your own, whenever they crop up. (If you need further assistance, you can always refer to this book—or dig into *Emily Post's Etiquette*, which addresses every situation under the sun.)

Bottom line: etiquette isn't about rules, it isn't stuffy, and it's not old-fashioned. Etiquette is a code of treating people with—and making choices based on—consideration, respect, and honesty. When you apply these principles consistently, etiquette becomes a tool that lets you build better relationships and be more successful in every aspect of your life.

Etiquette is not about doing what's "correct." Etiquette is about doing what's *right*.

Emily Post on Consideration

Emily Post knew that if you took an imaginary set of scales and balanced all of the rules of etiquette on one side and the principles of consideration, respect, and honesty on the other, the side with the principles would far outweigh the side with the manners.

Here's what she had to say about consideration:

Consideration for the rights and feelings of others is not merely a rule for behavior in public but the very foundation upon which social life is built.

The first rule of etiquette—which hundreds of others merely paraphrase or explain or elaborate—is:

Never do anything that is unpleasant to others.

PART ONE

....

Daily Life

1

····································

The Top Three Issues in Daily Life

THE ART OF ETIQUETTE really comes down to being thoughtful of the other people you encounter in your everyday life. We all tend to associate "proper behavior" with formal social events—but true etiquette involves behaving with respect and consideration for others in everything that you do, from attending a high-society soiree to simply hanging out around the house.

In fact, daily life is where men tend to run into more trouble than anywhere else. When the 750 women who responded to our recent Post Survey came to the question "What are the most annoying things men do in their daily lives?" we got quite an earful.

Here's a summary of the three main areas that our female respondents identified as their top hot-button issues when it comes to men and their everyday behavior:

Manners Matter

Opening doors. Putting down the toilet seat. Being on time. Not spitting. Taking off your hat indoors. Saying "Please" and "Thank you." Trying to be discreet and quiet when blowing your nose. These and other niceties may seem trivial to many men, but here's the scoop: *it all matters*. When you don't use the manners that people have come to expect—failing to open the door for a woman, for instance—it's not simply a sign that you're clueless; it shows a lack of consideration. *That's* what bothers women about men who don't have manners.

This brings us back to the essential guiding principle of this book: Good manners are *not* a matter of simply "following the rules." What's important is the *reason* underlying the desired behavior. Etiquette is about being considerate and honest with others. Manners matter, because manners are really about showing respect for another person. We hold the door for a woman not because there's a rule that says we should, but because it is an act of kindness and a way to make the woman you're with feel special. When you act in this spirit, she will know it and appreciate you for it. If you hold the door just because "that's the rule," she'll see right through you.

Helping Out Matters—A Lot

Here's a simple technique for driving a woman nuts: take the dishes to the sink—and then just leave them there. As one of our female respondents put it, "If you can carry them to the sink, why can't you take the time to put them in the dishwasher???"

According to the Post Survey, when it comes to helping out around the house, the modern male still has a long way to go. Those men who *do* help out at home scored higher in the category of *"pleasing* things that men do in their daily lives" than anything else, and by a wide margin. These men are role models for us all: they do the dishes, they do chores—without being asked. They do the "manly" jobs like washing the car, mowing the lawn, taking out the garbage—but they also help clean the house and do the laundry, and they don't leave a mess for someone else to pick up later. They clean up the counter and put away the fixings before they eat the sandwich they just made. They buy flowers "just because," or call her at work just to ask how she's doing. They give her compliments, unprompted. They hold hands. These guys are *really* good.

Why do women appreciate it so much? As our survey revealed, women perceive helping out as more than simply a matter of men doing their "assigned" chores or showing a little kindness. It's a matter of voluntarily taking responsibility and sharing the load.

Being Inconsiderate and Being Disrespectful Go Hand in Hand

Staring at other women. Talking down to women. Ignoring their opinions. Interrupting. Not introducing them. Simply ignoring them altogether. Walking several steps ahead of her rather than beside her. The Post Survey found that women don't simply view these behaviors as being rude or inconsiderate—to women, they represent a fundamental lack of personal respect.

To be fair, most men's "inconsiderate" or "disrespectful" behavior is not intentional. Men frequently get lost in their thoughts and go to far-off places in their minds without even realizing the journey has started, or considering the consequences. That's when they get into trouble.

Consider the issue of looking at another attractive woman who happens to cross your path. I do this unconsciously, I admit. But when my eyes stop looking at my wife's, and my attention shifts away just as she is making an important point, she views this as a case of my not being attentive to her. And she's right—my attention *has* wandered. Whenever a man "switches off" his thinking or wanders off on a mind journey, he runs the risk of looking inconsiderate and, by extension, disrespectful.

On a personal note, it scares me when I see what I've just written because I see some of myself in this description, and unfortunately it's not the good part. How long has it been since I made the bed in the morning? Why didn't I do those dishes from last night's dinner that were piled in the sink? After all, she made dinner. The least I could have done was clean up afterward. And I can't remember the last time I bought my wife flowers. Instead, I've been heard at the supermarket bemoaning the fact that she's picking out flowers and buying them for herself. Talk about clueless!

Now, I'm not *all* bad. I do clean any dishes still left in the sink each morning. I do remember to leave the toilet seat down. And I make coffee every morning and bring it to my wife in bed. In fact, our survey suggests that this last good deed may be the single "little thing" where American men excel the most: it's amazing how many men bring coffee or tea to their significant other in the morning.

Here's the bottom line: men get it right some of the time, but they don't generally spend enough effort really thinking through how their actions will affect the people around them. And *that's* what good etiquette really is: thinking about what the considerate, respectful thing to do would be, and then doing it. By thinking about our behavior, we turn each action into a conscious choice. The more we practice making those choices, the more often we'll make good choices—and the better our lives and the lives of our loved ones will be.

And that's what makes etiquette worth the effort.

2

....

Two Rooms That Can Make or Break Your Home Life

REMEMBER THAT DAY WHEN you moved into the first place of your own? You were the king of your castle: nobody to answer to, nobody to share chores with. You could watch the TV shows you wanted to watch, eat the foods you wanted to eat, and clean up or not. What a great setup!

It's also usually a very temporary state of affairs. One day—sooner than they might have imagined—most men wake up to find themselves married or living with a significant other or roommate. And whenever living space is shared, differences of opinion inevitably arise over the care and use of those spaces. These differences can turn into conflicts, if not handled thoughtfully.

Fortunately, the complexities of thoughtful home etiquette can be vastly simplified by thinking of your house as a series of discrete spaces—each with its own set of issues. Keep these key issues firmly in mind, and life will be blissfully peaceful on the home front.

In our Post Survey, we asked which shared spaces have the most potential to cause conflicts. Two rooms topped the list: the kitchen and the bathroom. Let's consider each in turn:

Clean Kitchen, Warm Heart

When we asked women to identify the leading cause of conflict in the kitchen, they gave one overwhelming answer: men don't do their share when it comes to cleaning up, especially after themselves.

I admit to being a primary offender in this regard. I used to drive my wife nuts on Saturday afternoons: I'd wander into the kitchen, and out would come all the fixings for a delectable Dagwood sandwich. The problem was, after making my sandwich, I wanted to eat it then and there. I'd sit right down at the kitchen table or, worse still, carry my creation into the living room to watch whatever sports happened to be on TV and munch away.

After a few minutes of this, my wife would wander in and invariably ask the same question: Why couldn't I clean up my mess *before* eating my sandwich?

The answer seemed obvious to me. "After all that work to make the sandwich, I want to eat it *now*," I would point out *reasonably*.

"What about the mess in the kitchen?"

Oh, that. "I'll get to it during halftime, or whatever," I'd mumble, guiltily tucking back into my sandwich.

In my interviews and speeches about etiquette, I talk quite a bit about how sincerity is an integral component in building relationships. Looking back on this particular scenario, I realize now that my sincerity quotient was in the cellar. My wife had seen those sandwich fixings stay out on the counter time and again. She knew (and, deep down, so did I) that I was only kidding myself; I would never get around to cleaning up my mess, and she was going to end up doing it instead.

Then, one Saturday, I had a breakthrough moment. Maybe the above scene had finally been repeated one too many times, or maybe the game of the week just wasn't very appealing that day—but for some reason, as I was making my sandwich in my usual fashion (as fast as possible, so I could get in front of the TV before the game started), the memory of my wife's words somehow penetrated my food- and football-fixated mind. To my own amazement, I actually stopped dead in my tracks and *put all the sandwich fixings away* before I started to eat.

I wish I could tell you exactly what prompted this revelation. All I know is that my wife's pleasure at my newfound sense of responsibility was and is palpable—and our life, inside and out of the kitchen, has improved because of it.

Of course, my sandwich is a metaphor for all of the important activity that goes on in a kitchen. The kitchen really is the soul of the home. It's where the family's meals are prepared, and often eaten. It's the room that requires the most cooperation to keep it clean and functioning.

For my wife and me, the key to harmony in the kitchen is a clear division of the chores. When we try to cook together, for example, we can't seem to avoid bumping into each other. Of course, we're also both geniuses at preparing chicken tarragon, and neither of us can stand seeing the other do it in anything less than *the* perfect way. After talking over the problem, we came up with a compromise: depending on the night and the menu, one of us does the cooking, and the other tackles the cleanup. Result: harmony.

When it comes to holding up your end of the kitchen duties, there are three simple keys:

1. *Pitch in consistently to clean up any general mess that accumulates.* This applies to cleaning up after meals, and also putting away all the junk that simply piles up during the day: groceries, mail, coats, boots, hats, gloves, towels, and sandals. Somehow this stuff seems to grow on its own in the kitchen. The spouse, significant other, or roommate who is left to deal with this alone must feel like the mythological Sisyphus, eternally doomed to push a huge rock up a hill only to watch it roll back down again. If you share a space with a roommate, Sisyphus won't remain your roommate for very long if he or she has to pick up your mess.

2. *Take personal responsibility for your own mess.* When you make or do anything that involves food or any other kitchen supplies—like my Dagwood sandwich—*clean it up as soon as possible.*

3. *Complete all kitchen chores.* Men often think that where kitchen chores are concerned, half a loaf is better than none. I'm as guilty as the next guy: I would much rather leave the just-washed dinner dishes dripping in the dish rack than dry them and put them away. This half-loaf philosophy is one that particularly drives women crazy (if you don't believe it, ask your wife or girlfriend). It's *not* enough to bring the groceries in from the

SURVEY SAYS

Make the Bedroom a "Safe Zone"

Interestingly, while other rooms seem to be rife with issues, many of our survey respondents described their bedrooms as a "safe zone"—a place where they and their spouses consciously agree to leave arguments behind. Instead, it's reserved as a space where they can share intimacy and be together and be safe in their togetherness.

"Fortunately, we don't have problems here," wrote one respondent. "We both respect each other's space and we usually enjoy spending time in this room."

"Never fight in the bedroom," added another. "It sours the sex." A third survey-taker reported, "No problems in the bedroom. It is as if it is a restful sanctuary and we respect that."

I like that concept—respect for the space, and respect for each other within the space. Not that the bedroom is completely issue-free, of course. Snoring, blanket hogging, and lack of personal hygiene came up repeatedly in the Post Survey as behaviors that can lead to conflict in the bedroom. One sin of omission took the cake, however: leaving dirty clothes around. So remember, to keep harmony in your bedroom, put your dirty clothes where they belong—in the clothes hamper. Better yet, learn how to operate that washer and dryer or take a load to the laundromat yourself. Her gratitude will know no bounds.

car and then leave them on the counter, or to rinse the dishes, then stack them to be washed "later." Once you've started a job, *finish it.*

The Battle of the Bathroom

The bathroom is the one place where we all truly want to be private and comfortable. In an ideal world, everyone would have a bathroom that was theirs and theirs alone. In reality, however, most of us share a bathroom with a significant other, and perhaps with other family members or roommates. This overlap of personal space is where the troubles start.

For men, the most important thing to understand is that women tend to be very particular about the bathroom. This leads to a major truth that men are best off simply accepting: *the bathroom is her domain.* You, the man, are essentially a visitor. If you don't believe me, just look at the "stuff" in your own bathroom. In my case, my "stuff" takes up part of one drawer. Hers takes up the rest of the room.

That's why, when it comes to bathroom behavior, it's almost always a good idea to be accommodating of your partner's needs and desires. This delicate area is generally *not* the place to make a stand on some point of personal self-expression.

Here are the "hot spots" to watch out for in any bathroom:

The Sink

One of the problems with shaving is that it's messy, at least if you use shaving cream and a manual razor. When I got married, I quickly realized that even though I might not be bothered by that stubble in the sink, my wife did not share my view.

As a visitor to this room, it's your job to learn how to leave the sink—and the rest of the bathroom—in a condition suitable to the owner of the room. One easy way for me to avoid my wife's wrath is to spend a minute or so making sure the sink is cleaned of my shaving residue and ready for her use. I know that I'm not going to get rewarded, praised, or even acknowledged for this act—and that's not why I do it. I do it because I know she doesn't like it when she goes to use the sink and finds it full of my stubble.

In other words, it's the considerate thing to do.

One final sink tip: after I shave, there's always water left on the counter. I make sure I wipe this water up and leave the counter dry. Why? Because one day, when I didn't wipe it up, my wife came in after me and leaned against the counter so she could get a better look at herself in the mirror while she did her makeup. When she stepped away from the sink, her nice, white skirt had a big wet spot on it. I only made that mistake once.

The Bathtub/Shower

Bathtubs conjure up all sorts of lascivious images. Bubbles; an adventurous moment with your significant other or someone you're dreaming of; feet, legs, arms, hands all intertwined. It gets pretty good.

Dream on. I don't know about your setup, but our tub is five feet long, tops. If I ever did try to climb in with my wife, the faucet would leave a permanent impression on my back. Save that cuddling-in-the-bubble-bath stuff for your vacations in that hotel room with the tub as big as the Ritz. When it comes to the typical bathtub in the home, your thoughts should be confined to how you can keep it clean and attractive for your wife or girlfriend. I doubt that a roommate would want to clean up your mess, either.

Whether you have a stall shower or a bathtub that also doubles as a shower, have you noticed how the water often starts building up in the tub or stall while you're taking a shower? That slow-draining water is a clear indication that hair and soap scum are partially blocking the drain. This not only forces you and your partner to shower in ankle-deep water, but also leaves behind a dirty bathtub ring. The proper (and considerate) response is to immediately grab some toilet tissue and clear the drain, then grab a sponge and some cleanser, and make that bathtub ring disappear. (A consistently sluggish drain may be a sign that the trap is clogged as well, meaning that a superficial cleaning won't help. In this case, try some liquid drain cleaner. If that fails, it's time to grab your tool kit and give the trap a cleaning, or bite the bullet and call a plumber.)

"But it's mostly *her* hair," you argue. *It doesn't matter.* Just clean the drain out. You were the last one in the shower, so you own the problem, whether it's your fault or not.

The Toilet Seat

We now come to the all-important issue of the toilet seat. Here's the scenario: it's three in the morning, and your dream's been pretty good. But now you're awake, and you realize that you really need to go to the bathroom.

You carefully slip out of bed—woe to you if you wake her—and head into the bathroom with one thought: to get your business done and get back to bed. The problem is that now, at the ungodly hour of three A.M., you are facing a crucial etiquette challenge: remembering to put the toilet seat down.

Here are the two transgressions you can make in this befuddled state, in order of their seriousness:

TRANSGRESSION 1— You lift the toilet seat, do your business, and then pad back to bed *without putting the seat back down*. Maybe you just forgot. Or maybe you were feeling a little lazy. "It's only fair," you think to yourself. "I raised the seat—she can lower it."

It Could Happen to You

....

After a speech I gave recently, a couple of men voiced their skepticism about the importance of the toilet seat issue—until Sam, another attendee, told them his story:

In the middle of the night, Sam awoke and padded off to the bathroom. Unfortunately for him, on this particular night he needed to sit. "I had lowered myself about three quarters of the way when I realized the seat wasn't down," he recalls. "I didn't want to sit on the rim of the bowl, so I tried to stop in midair. I slipped. Before I knew it, I fell back against the toilet, crashing into the tank and smashing it to pieces. Water and shards of tank covered the floor. The mess was unbelievable."

Sam was lucky to emerge with only a bruised ego. Lesson learned the hard way: put the seat down.

....

Wrong. This issue has nothing to do with division of labor. When nature calls at an ungodly hour, and a woman settles sleepily into a sitting position, *she expects that seat to be down.* Anything other than that is a very rude surprise. Think about it: Would you like to sit on the rim?

TRANSGRESSION 2— You forget to put the seat up *before* relieving yourself. Remember, it's dark, you're sleepy, and even at high noon your aim isn't always perfectly true. If that seat isn't dry and clean as a whistle and your wife rises and heads to *the same toilet*, frankly, I can think of many other places I'd rather be.

Of course, you *know* the right thing to do in both situations. But merely *knowing* isn't enough. There are some tasks that men are absolutely required to perform in order to make life easier and more trouble free for everyone. This is one of them. Sometimes avoiding trouble is the best reason of all for doing the right thing.

Toilet Paper

No one should have to face this sort of thing first thing in the morning. Only two or three sheets were left on the roll. No spare was in sight, and my wife was blissfully asleep.

We all know what it feels like to be in that situation. As men, we should always make a point of knowing where the spare roll of toilet paper is kept, and bringing that spare roll within arm's reach whenever the current roll starts running low. (Many households keep a spare roll nearby at all times, in a knit cover or in some other convenient container.)

Even better: when the roll actually runs out, don't rely on your wife to pop the new roll into the dispenser, but play the unsung hero and do it yourself.

Personal-Care Items

The bathroom is also the ultimate domestic litmus test for how well you and your partner respect each other's "things" and each other's privacy.

Take toothbrushes, for instance. My toothbrush is *mine*—it's got my own personal germs on it, and I don't want anyone else's joining them there. Your significant other may feel the same way I do. If you suddenly discover you can't find your own toothbrush, before going ahead and grabbing your wife's you should consider exactly how she's going to feel about someone else using her toothbrush. Even if you really think she won't mind, the considerate thing to do is to *check anyway* by asking her. A trip to an all-night drugstore or missing one night's brushing is better than time spent patching bruised feelings.

The same goes for all other personal-care products, including hairbrushes, razors, lotions, and deodorants. Take the time to fully acquaint yourself with your partner's personal idiosyncrasies in these areas, and respect his or her preferences at all times. Sometimes it's better not to "share."

Privacy

The subject of bathroom privacy is more delicate and somewhat more abstract than other bathroom etiquette issues, but it's no less important. When you're living alone, you can leave the door open while you do whatever is necessary and it won't change the universe one bit. Once you begin living in a shared space, however, a closed door becomes important. This is true when you are using the bathroom yourself, and even more true when your partner is using it. A closed door is an unspoken request for privacy, and it should be honored at all times.

3

Other Household Hot Spots

THE KEY TO A peaceful, happy home life (besides watching your step in the kitchen and the bathroom) is to pay special attention to the "hot spots" that tend to crop up on any given day. Our Post Survey respondents identified three key issues as the ones most likely to cause problems in day-to-day life:

> ➤ Sharing household chores

> ➤ Watching television

> ➤ Dealing with the telephone

What also came across in their descriptions of these hot spots was the overwhelming sense of frustration that women feel about how clueless men can be. All too often, we men are simply not aware of how our actions affect the people around us. It's that altered mind state we get into.

Fortunately, etiquette provides a roadmap back to reality when our minds wander. Etiquette is really a set of clues for building solid, respectful relationships—and whenever you share a living space with other people, you are, de facto, in a relationship, since everything you do affects them as well. What these other people generally want is for you to respect them and the efforts they are making to render the space livable, and to contribute a like amount of effort yourself.

Seeing the Man in the Mirror

Mud season in Vermont is a vile time of year. A typical rule in our home could well be "Wipe your feet before coming into the house." But the fact is, it *really doesn't matter* if I wipe my feet when I come inside with muddy boots on. What matters is that I notice the muddy trail I've made, and that I then clean it up. When I do this, I'm being considerate and aware of how my actions affect someone else—namely my wife, who cleaned the floor and would like it to stay clean. If I choose not to wipe my feet every time I enter the house, so be it—provided I also take responsibility for cleaning up the mess I've made.

My muddy boots are a metaphor for a larger truth: by holding up a mirror to my own behavior, I am able to turn a potentially difficult situation into a no-brainer. We all have to learn to keep one eye on this mental mirror and see ourselves as others see us. This means being conscious at all times of how our actions affect others.

Sharing the Load

Congratulations! In the Post Survey, we men get high marks for mowing the lawn. There must be any number of men who view this chore as making up their entire, 50 percent contribution to the job of running the household. The problem is, there's a lot more to managing a house than mowing the lawn. Here are just some of the other daily chores respondents cited:

Laundry	Vacuuming
Housework	Taking out the garbage
Ironing	Changing lightbulbs
Baby watching	Doing the grocery shopping
Cooking	Paying the bills
Making the bed(s)	Planning an evening out

Planning an Evening Out

....

Our survey got reams of comments about how men never lift a finger to figure out what the couple is going to do on a date. All I know is that when I plan a date with my wife, it has a superb effect on her.

Recently, we went on a cruise with her entire family. It really turned out great—despite what you're thinking. The cruise departed from New York City at two P.M. on a Saturday afternoon. Plotting with my wife's older brother, I found a low-cost air fare from Burlington to New York and got tickets to *Mamma Mia!* (a fabulous Broadway play) for the Friday night before our departure. We had a great dinner before the show, and even managed a limo ride back to her brother's house afterward. Admittedly, that's a pretty extravagant date—but it was a great evening and all she had to do was be there and enjoy.

On other occasions, I'll suggest we eat out—and then call the restaurant to make a reservation. When we still had baby-sittable kids, my arranging for the sitter would be the absolute icing on the cake.

....

When it comes to chores around the house, very often we'll identify something specific we want to get done together. We might spend Saturday morning cleaning out the office or repainting the front hall or cleaning out the refrigerator (it's frightening that our fridge can get so bad it takes a whole morning to clean it out). That leaves Saturday afternoon for golf, skiing, or whatever. The key is that we tackle the chore together, and we plan something fun to do afterward. That way, no one feels that they're left doing all the dirty work.

"What TV Show Are We Going to Watch?"

One Post Survey respondent defined this problem as "Lifetime versus Sportscenter." Another woman wrote, "Most people can only watch a John Wayne flick so many times." (Personally I disagree; I have yet to tire of watching the Duke.)

Just the other night, my wife and I were channel surfing the movies on our satellite system. "Debbie says that's a good movie," my wife announced suddenly when *Monsoon Wedding* popped up as one of the selections. "It's a chick flick," she added, and we passed it by without further comment.

The way our arrangement works, there are "her" shows, "my" shows, and "our" shows. Some day in the near future I'll be either on the road or at a hockey game, and she can catch *Monsoon Wedding* then. The same goes for me: I'll save *Fort Apache* for some time when my wife is either out or not interested in watching. Even if you don't have a satellite system or cable that repeats the show over and over again, the key is to recognize it's "our" house and "our" living room—and that we both need to compromise when watching "our" television together.

The second most difficult conflict caused by the TV involves the ownership of the remote control. I have a good friend who literally keeps the remotes tied next to "his" recliner in the living room. Ostensibly this is to prevent the dreaded misplacement of the remote, but it also places the clicker conveniently under his control.

I think my wife wonders whether I simply use the remote to see how fast I can click through the channels. As any true remote control junkie knows, if you click fast enough you can actually watch two or three shows simultaneously. How your viewing partner feels about watching this sort of triple feature is another matter.

Lately, I've been learning to slow down or, better yet—horror of horrors for anyone with a pathological need to control the remote—even offer my wife the clicker on occasion.

"Here, honey, you find something," I say as sweetly as I can.

"No, no, no," she always replies, pushing it away as if it's cursed.

This is admittedly a risky strategy, because you've got to be prepared for those times when the other person actually does take control. The upside is that this approach puts a stop to any arguing about the remote.

The bottom line: television viewing should be relaxing for everyone. To keep it from becoming adversarial, think before you act and be considerate by taking into account everyone's interests.

The Telephone

The telephone is a diabolical technological invention. You can't live without it, but you can't succeed with it—at least, not if you believe what the Post Survey respondents have to say about the phone. For them, misuse of the telephone falls into three very clear-cut categories: not answering the phone, not using the phone, and failing to take messages.

Not Answering the Phone

It's the stuff of television sitcoms. Scene: the male character is lounging on the couch, watching something on TV, when the phone rings. The phone is usually about ten feet away.

"Honey, can you get that?" the man shouts.

Honey trudges up the basement stairs carrying a load of laundry and, huffing and puffing, answers the phone. "Keep it down, will you?" her husband yells. "I'm trying to watch the game here."

Unfortunately, TV sitcoms often parody real life.

Bottom line: when the phone rings, answer it.

Not Using the Phone

Typically, problems with the phone are associated with the abuse of using it. But men have mastered a whole other side of phone misbehavior: *not* using it at the most inappropriate times.

"Call me if you're going to be late," my wife would ask as I got ready to head out the door on the way to work. She may be trying to time dinner so it'll be ready when I get home. Or she may have errands, work, or children's events to coordinate. Or she may simply worry that something has happened to me if I don't arrive when I'm expected.

It seems like a reasonable request. The problem is, I have failed to make that call a few thousand times. Eventually, by the time cell phones were invented, I learned to call whenever I was leaving wherever I was.

Peace.

Not Taking Messages

Taking messages can be a pain in the neck. Let's say I'm up to my elbows in sawdust, working on a project in my shop. My wife isn't home. The kids aren't home. The phone rings. Now, I'm no good at letting the answering machine pick up. Technology has defeated me: I *must* answer that phone.

It's for my wife. "I'll let her know you called," I promise, dropping the phone into its cradle and rushing back downstairs to finish marking the wood for the next cut. Measure twice, cut once. I'm completely focused on my project.

Sure, I'll remember to tell her about the call. And it snows in July in Vermont occasionally, too.

In the grand scheme of things—such as world peace, or solving the problems of starvation and overpopulation—actions like taking a phone message don't seem all that important. The fact is, however, etiquette isn't about momentous acts. It is about smoothing the way through life for ourselves and the people around us.

That's why taking a message becomes important. It's one act in a continuum of actions that cumulatively make a difference. By doing it and doing it well, we are able to reach out and help another person.

So in spite of my annoyance at the interruption, I grab a piece of paper and jot the message down: name, number, time of call, and the message.

When You're Not the Problem

Now, maybe you're thinking to yourself, "None of this advice so far applies to *me!*"

Okay, let's suppose you're the type of thoughtful person who never fails to clean the sink or pick up your dirty clothes. In fact, you're fastidious—it's the *other* person who is the problem. In this case, you have two options.

Option Number One

Do nothing. Particularly with a wife or live-in significant other, this is often the best policy. Example: throughout thirty years of marriage, my wife has buried the armchair in our bedroom under her clothes. It's been so well covered for so long that I no longer have any clear idea of the color of the chair's fabric. Now, I'm no neat-freak. Anyone who has ever seen my office knows this. But somehow I've developed the habit of putting my dirty clothes in the hamper every morning, and putting away my other clothes in the bureau or the closet. (Actually I do this primarily out of self-interest: we've divided chores and my wife does the laundry—so by making sure my clothes are where they are meant to be, I'm ensuring that they get cleaned.)

Anyway, the one thing I don't *ever* do is say a word to my wife about the pile of clothes on the chair. This is simply not an issue I care to expend any built-up goodwill capital on. Besides, the upholstery has lasted an incredibly long time—no doubt due to the fact that the chair gets virtually no use, and no light can shine through to fade the fabric. Here's to the chair: may it last another thirty years!

Option Number Two

Try to change your housemate's offending behavior. This is ticklish work, to say the least. Anytime you choose to talk to someone about what you perceive to be their failings, they tend to become very defensive, very quickly. Before you pursue this option, go back and carefully reconsider Option Number One. Ask yourself: Is this issue *really* worth stirring the pot over?

If you do decide to plunge ahead with your behavior modification project, remember that your goal in attempting to change someone else's behavior should always be to build a better relationship with that person, not simply to be critical for its own sake.

4

How Others View Us

MY TYPICAL SATURDAY MORNING goes something like this: the sun is shining, the lawn needs mowing, the oil in my car has to be changed, and there are ten other chores that need attention after that. In this situation, I often don't shower or shave. I just throw on a T-shirt and jeans, and I'm ready for the day.

What I'm saying is that it's okay to be a little grubby on Saturday mornings—as long as you're tinkering on your own, or running errands to the hardware store or the grocery store. But this permissiveness has its limits: when the phone rings and friends ask us to join them for lunch, I know I'm going to have to hit the shower, shave, and put some clean clothes on. The same holds true if my wife says, "Peter, let's go to the movies later," or if the dinner hour rolls around and I'm still immersed in chores. There's no question that I've got to be cleaned up, shaved, combed, dressed nicely, and smelling good by the time we leave the house or sit down at the dinner table.

When I'm in close quarters with anyone, I want to be attractive, not repulsive. This is true whether I'm with my wife, or I'm attending a religious service, or have a social engagement with friends, or a weekend meeting planned with business colleagues.

Friends, Foes, and the Baseball Cap

In the Middle Ages, knights in shining armor would meet each other covered from head to toe in armor. Often they simply could not be identified and had no idea if the other knight was friend or foe. So they took to lifting their helmets off to reveal their identities to each other. The servers at banquets in the Middle Ages were required to remove their hats as a mark of deference to the patrons. The removing of a head covering became a custom and evolved into the removal of a hat being a mark of respect. This action has remained a custom ever since.

When you enter a person's home, removing your hat is a symbol of your respect for the owner. Likewise, as you enter a restaurant, taking off your cap is the right thing to do for the people you are with and for the other diners. Any time you enter a place of religion, your baseball cap should come off. However, when you enter a store or other public space, you can keep your cap on.

Each of us is responsible for how others view us. Taking that responsibility seriously is a clear signal of your respect for others. If you choose to go on a date without cleaning up first, *you* are responsible when your date decides she doesn't want to see you again. Pass gas or let loose with a string of expletives when you're with a group of friends, and they may forgive one episode—but make it a habit, and you could quickly find yourself without friends.

I didn't pick these examples at random. When we asked our Post Survey respondents to tell us where men are most likely to have significant problems with their appearance and demeanor, failing to bathe, passing gas, and foul language all emerged as major issues—as did smoking, chewing gum, and spitting.

Judging by these survey results, there are far too many guys out there seemingly stuck in Saturday-morning mode all week long. To help make sure you're not one of them, here's a quick rundown on each of these key issues:

Hygiene

The best way to deal with hygiene is to wash daily, and brush your teeth morning and night. Do the same before any date or other important get-together. If there's *any chance* you could be offensive, take action!

Some men are selective about their hygiene habits: they allow themselves to go unwashed or have bad breath at home, but not when they go out. After all, there's no etiquette rule that says it's okay to drop your standards at home.

Now comes the hard part. How can you tell if you have body odor or bad breath, or if you're using too much cologne, or your antiperspirant really smells worse than nothing at all? You can't judge these things for yourself, because you're too familiar with the smells to notice them. The problem is that if you *are* an offender, most people are far too uncomfortable about the subject to ever bring it up on their own.

This is a shame, because at heart we're all begging to be apprised of the truth. In my seminars, I always ask, "How many people here would prefer it if a friend tells you if you have body odor or bad breath?" Whenever I pose this question, virtually every hand in the room goes up.

Fortunately, there's a solution to this dilemma: place a friendly inquiry with a friend, a roommate, your spouse, or your significant other. If you *ask* them, then they have permission to speak.

"Tom, we've been sharing this apartment for a couple of months, and I've got to ask you something. I know it's going to sound weird, but I want to be sure because I really don't want to be grossing you out. Do I

SURVEY SAYS
What Women *Really* Think About Men and Hygiene

"Clean hair and nails are a must; a well-groomed man is very sexy!"

"They have a lack of personal hygiene—especially ear hair or nose hair."

"Soap and water are cheap enough for everyone to be clean."

"How come men get away with not shaving for days?"

"It takes fifteen seconds to look in the mirror and determine your appearance."

"Smelling of stale smoke on clothing and breath."

"Bad sanitary habits—they don't shower enough."

"Teeth and hair are very important; if you can't take care of your own teeth, I can't imagine what else you must not be taking care of."

have bad breath? Have you ever noticed it? Because if you have, I want to do something about it."

If you don't have bad breath, Tom simply says so. End of story. If you *do* have bad breath, he will almost certainly feel an incredible sense of relief at finally being able to say something, without having to be the one who brought it up.

Smoking

Used to be, it was a smoker's world. You could light up with impunity just about anywhere—in an airplane, in a cab, at a restaurant, in a store, or in a person's home.

Not anymore. If you smoke, it's up to you to be aware of the rules in public places, and follow them. Nobody is impressed with a person who smokes where smoking is prohibited. When you visit another person's home, *never* light up in the home without asking permission first—and be prepared to step outside good-naturedly for your smoke, if your host requests it.

The smell of smoke on your clothes or in your car can be bothersome to others. Imagine spiffing yourself up for a hot date, cologne and all— then having a smoke before picking up your date. Greeting her with the aroma of tobacco clinging to you will be counterproductive, to say the least!

Sometimes, especially when cigars are involved, men forget that their exhaled smoke is generally viewed as obnoxious, invasive, and annoying. It's worth remembering that many people have an especially visceral reaction to cigar smoke.

If you do choose to puff a stogie in a private home or a public place that allows it, check with everyone in your group first to make sure no one minds—then offer cigars to anyone who wants one, including the women.

Chewing Gum

My good friend Becky was severely grossed out the other day. She was working the circuit at her gym, moving from one station to the next, when she saw it: there on the bench, where she was about to sit, was a sticky wad of chewing gum.

You have to wonder what goes through some people's minds.

Chewing gum is like using a cell phone—the only time it is appropriate is when you can do it without negatively affecting the people around you. Making cracking sounds, chewing it with your mouth open, or blowing bubbles are all revolting intrusions on the people around you. If you're in a theater, at a concert, working right next to another person, or standing in a crowded elevator or other public area, chew your gum silently with your mouth closed, if you must chew at all. And when you're on a date—whether it's a first date or a night out with your spouse or significant other—forget the gum completely.

Spitting

Most men are pretty adept at spitting. In junior high, we used to have contests to see who could spit the farthest. Of course, back then, we also didn't worry too much about what the girls thought. Today, in adulthood, it's different. And women put spitting high on the list of things men do that truly annoy them.

To be sure, there's a difference between spitting on an athletic field and letting fly as you're walking arm-in-arm with your date. The trick is to avoid letting your behavior when you're alone, on the athletic field, or hanging out with the guys turn into a habitual action that you do without thinking, even when you are with a woman or in polite company.

For starters, when you're with other people and need to clear your throat, excuse yourself and take care of your business in private. If you can't excuse yourself, discreetly spit into a paper tissue and dispose of it.

Be a Hero—Carry a Pack of Tissues

Carrying a small pack of tissues in your pocket at all times is one of the simplest and most valuable pieces of etiquette advice you'll ever hear. Having a tissue handy does more than ensure you'll always be able to take care of your needs— you'll also be a lifesaver for those less-prepared folks who suddenly need to sneeze.

"Here, have a tissue," you can offer politely. Suddenly, you're a hero!

Handkerchiefs vs. Tissues

With the strength and quality of facial tissues these days, I recommend keeping your handkerchief as a fashion statement, and leaving it at that. Putting your used handkerchief in your pocket is bad enough, but imagine handing it to someone else to use!

Passing Gas

Another rite of passage for adolescent boys is learning how to pass gas for maximum effect. While this talent might have wowed your thirteen-year-old buddies, it will not impress the adults around you—particularly the women. In our Post Survey, one out of six respondents indicated that passing gas was one of the "things men do that really annoy women."

What do you do if you're on a date and you've got to pass gas?

My answer: What do you do if you have to go to the bathroom? The principle is the same. You can retire briefly to the bathroom, or hold it in. If for some reason you absolutely can't excuse yourself and you can't hold it any longer, then let it pass as discreetly as possible—and be prepared to own up and apologize, if necessary.

Swearing

My wife knows music. The kids all love to talk with her because she's up on all the latest groups. The other day she left a CD in my truck. Shawn Colvin. Shawn's a she, in case you didn't know. Nice sound. Great voice. So we're out driving around, doing errands, when suddenly my ears start ringing. "F—— off!" sings Shawn, clear as day.

That's when it hit me: swearing jars the listener when it's not expected. And when a person swears, the listener's attention shifts from what the speaker is saying to the word(s) that startled them.

Etiquette Imperative

....

Curb your swearing. When you swear, the listener doesn't focus on what you are saying but rather on how you are saying it.

....

Basically, swearing is a cultural issue. Certain groups may be comfortable with the use of certain words, while other groups may find the same words offensive. For example, I was recently asked to do a seminar for a national company with two distinct cultures—a "Southern" culture and a "Northeast" culture. The firm's Northeast workers have a habit of swearing in their business conversations, while the Southern employees never use profanity. As a result, the Southern people feel very uncomfortable when talking to their Northeast colleagues.

People also have different opinions about what constitutes swearing. That's why I always try to keep colorful language out of my presentations; I don't want to risk offending any participants, and the use of swear words isn't going to enhance my message one bit. At a recent seminar in Dallas, however, in my excitement at responding to a participant's comments, I involuntarily exclaimed, "Oh, my god!" I didn't think twice about it—the phrase just rolled out. Later, while reading through the seminar evaluations, I was surprised to find a comment criticizing me for taking the Lord's name in vain. In some places, my choice of words wouldn't have raised an eyebrow. To this person, however, they were deeply offensive.

Bottom line: being careful to choose our words so we don't offend our listeners is a lesson we all need to periodically relearn. Even when you're with a group of friends accustomed to using profanity, if you think that someone—anyone—in the group might be bothered by it, then be considerate and hold your tongue. And if you're not sure . . . hold it anyway.

5

....

A Man and His Car

IT'S FIVE FORTY-FIVE P.M., THE end of a long day, and I'm glad to be on the way home. Country roads in Vermont are beautiful, and I'm looking forward to a relaxing drive. Then I see it—a drab, ten-year-old sedan, crawling along the road in front of me. The speed limit is a mere thirty-five miles per hour, and this guy's barely doing thirty. Traffic's coming the other way, and I'm trapped: I have to brake.

I'm so close I can't see the road between me and him, and I can feel the rush of adrenaline. *"Come on idiot, move it!"* I snarl to myself. After a couple of minutes of this, believe it or not, he starts *slowing down*. Meanwhile my blood pressure is moving just as quickly in the opposite direction. A right turn's coming up, we're down to ten miles per hour, and I'm boiling over with impatience. Just as he starts to turn, he finally switches on his blinker.

I squeeze by, hit the accelerator, and roar past his receding rear end, thinking, "That showed him." A mile later I turn onto the dirt road where I live, and before I know it I'm home—still hyped from the adrenaline rush from my encounter.

According to the experts, I'm now officially one of the 35 percent of Americans who admit to engaging in an act of road rage. The next time you're on the road, look around you and think of that statistic: one out of every three drivers *admits* being guilty of road rage, and the true figure is probably higher. In fact, six out of ten people surveyed say they often see drivers who are acting aggressively or recklessly.

I wasn't as bad as I might have been—after all, I didn't yell, curse (not so the driver could hear me, anyway), or worse. Still, with the benefit of hindsight, I can count several aggressive behaviors in my one brief encounter: tailgating; unnecessarily abrupt speed change; lost temper; and venting my frustration verbally.

Road rage, aggressive behavior—call it what you will—is dangerous, it's foolish, and it doesn't get you anywhere. As it turns out, I got home one or two minutes later than I would have otherwise. Big deal. If I had simply done a few deep-breathing exercises and kept calm instead of overreacting, I would have arrived home relaxed and serene rather than tense and fuming.

While you're never going to be able to control how others act in their cars, you *can* start changing your own road rage behavior. The first essential step is to recognize that you're engaging in this type of behavior. Ask yourself:

➤ Am I screaming at other drivers?

➤ Do I think of my vehicle as a weapon of revenge?

➤ Am I *always* right and the other driver *always* wrong?

➤ Do I sense that my blood pressure is rising rapidly during a frustrating encounter on the road?

The next step is to work on developing a different response to situations that ordinarily would get you fuming. Slow down, take a deep breath or three, and yield to the other driver. If not for yourself, then at least do it for the others close to you, for the people in the other car, and for your children who will be driving themselves one day.

Your goal: consciously work at being considerate of the people in your car and in the cars around you. That's how to combat road rage.

Of course, this process takes time. I'm working hard on it, but I still catch myself muttering under my breath or casting the evil eye at a particularly foolish driver. Overall, though, my attitude *is* getting better. For instance, I no longer do the tailgating trick to force a slow car in front of me to go faster. (It doesn't work, anyway.)

Aggressive Driving Is Turnoff Number One

In the Post Survey, when we asked women to identify the most annoying things men do in a car, fully 50 percent of our respondents said they were bothered most by men who behaved aggressively—by driving too fast, tailgating other cars, yelling, swearing, making rude gestures, weaving in and out of traffic, and cutting other drivers off.

Driver's Ed-iquette

While road rage is the most dramatic example of inconsiderate driving, there are other key behaviors that the Thinking Man should also keep in mind at all times:

Use Your Blinkers

It's amazing how many people fail to use their blinkers properly. If that guy in the ten-year-old sedan had flashed his signal to let me know he was slowing down to turn, maybe I wouldn't have been up his tailpipe.

Signaling all turns well ahead of time is the courteous—and safe—thing to do. The same goes for using your blinker to indicate when you're changing lanes on the highway. (In most states it's also required by law.)

Learn to Distinguish Between Helpful Observations vs. Backseat Driving

There's a difference between a legitimate warning—"Careful, there's a car pulling out of that driveway"—and unsolicited advice like:

"You're shifting at the wrong time. Do you want to ruin the clutch?"

"Don't you know how to start up a hill?"

"You should be in the right lane."

"You can pass. Go, *now!*"

Leave backseat driving behind: the driver doesn't appreciate it, and it is dangerously distracting. Close your mouth and let the driver drive. You and everyone else in the car will be safer and happier because of your restraint.

Sometimes you may find yourself the victim of backseat driving. The other day, for example, my wife and I were driving to our yoga class at

The Horn-y Pick-up

One situation where gratuitous horn-blowing is particularly inconsiderate is when you arrive in a car to pick up your date. Rule of thumb: *no horns*. Start the evening right by getting out of your car, walking up to the front door, and knocking. No woman is going to be impressed (let alone flattered) by the beckoning call of a car horn.

five-thirty A.M., while it was still dark out. "Do you see those joggers?" she asked. They were carrying flashlights. How could I possibly *not* see them?

"Yes, thank you," I responded politely. And therein lies the key for responding to backseat driving. Take a deep breath and don't overreact. Your job as the driver is to keep your focus on the road, regardless of the actions of the people around you.

Use the Horn Only When Absolutely Necessary

Contrary to what many people believe, the car horn was not designed as an accessory for attracting attention, for expressing your impatience or frustration with the traffic jam you're stuck in, or for tooting hello to your buddies. Your horn is there to sound an alarm and give warning to other drivers. That's why it's designed to be loud and obtrusive. Honking your horn for any reason other than pure safety considerations is inconsiderate.

Male Critics Drive Women Nuts

Women become particularly frustrated by the male belief that women don't know how to drive. Survey respondents vented their frustration in the following comments:

"They act superior—put down every woman driver."

"They can't stand to let a woman drive while they are in the car."

"He criticizes me on my driving habits."

"They treat women like they are inferior drivers."

"He always says: 'It *must* be a *woman* driving that car.' "

If you see this attitude of male supremacy in yourself, be aware it isn't winning you any points in the game of life. Take a deep breath, and try sitting back and enjoying the ride.

"Don't Worry—I Know How to Get There."

We were newly arrived in Orlando, and my friend Paul was driving a rental car packed with ourselves, our wives, and our golf clubs. It was about eight o'clock in the evening, and Paul knew about a steakhouse he wanted us to enjoy. His wife suggested he get directions, but he responded with those famous last words that every man has uttered at least once:

"Don't worry, honey; I know how to get there."

We made a few turns, then a few U-turns, and finally ended up heading several miles in absolutely the wrong direction. Fortunately Paul's unerring sense of direction turned us around one more time, and after back tracking, we finally caught sight of a landmark or two. Up on the left in the next strip mall, there it was. We'd made it. The journey took twice as long as it should have, but at least we men had the satisfaction of having never looked at a map or asked for directions. By the way, the steak *was* really good.

We got lucky that evening. But if we had truly wanted to be considerate of our wives—and ourselves, for that matter—we would have taken a minute to call the steakhouse and get directions. That way we could have relaxed and concentrated on the nice meal ahead of us.

It's a funny thing about men and directions. The results of the Post Survey indicate that men really don't like to ask for directions, and women really don't like getting lost. In fact, men's reluctance to ask for directions was the third most common "annoying car behavior" cited by our women respondents, after aggressive driving and speeding.

What the "asking directions" issue is really about is letting go of your male ego and surrendering to the fact that it's not a loss of face to ask someone for help. In fact, the alternative may leave you looking pretty foolish. As a bonus, you'll find that if you trust in people, this trust will often be repaid in surprising ways.

To illustrate this point, consider another very different episode. One year, when my wife and I were on our annual trip to Italy, we found ourselves trying to navigate the mountain pass leading to the famed Amalfi Coast. The road up the pass is one of the world's truly great switchback roads, with magnificent views of Mount Vesuvius and the Italian coast around every turn.

The trouble was, after driving for quite some time, we were nowhere near the crest. Instead, we were hopelessly lost in Pagani. All we knew was that we must've missed a turn. Reluctantly, I pulled into a gas station to— you guessed it—*ask for directions*. The only saving grace for my male ego was the fact that my wife speaks Italian. She got out to ask directions. Whenever a good-looking woman approaches a cluster of Italian men and asks for help, a great discussion ensues. Finally, she came back to the car.

"Follow that man and his son," she said, pointing to two members of the group who were getting into a car. "They're going to lead us to the road we're looking for." We followed their car through a bewildering number of turns along the back roads of the town. Never in a hundred years would we have found the way on our own. Then the car suddenly pulled to the shoulder, and the man waved us on. "Turn right at the next intersection and just follow that road," he instructed.

I never got the chance to thank our guide and his son for going so far out of their way to help two Americans lost on the way to Amalfi. If they happen to read this: *Grazie mille*.

6

Communication

"WHAT WE HAVE HERE is failure to communicate." The captain of the prison road gang in the movie *Cool Hand Luke* may have been a bit on the sadistic side, but he understood what it takes to make a relationship work. Look at any relationship that's in trouble, and it's a good bet the underlying problem can be traced to a *failure to communicate*.

These days, there are more *ways* to communicate than ever before: in person, over the telephone, via voice mail or e-mail—or even by writing someone a letter (for those of us who still get special enjoyment from sending and receiving snail mail).

But simply having these tools in your toolbox isn't enough. You have to know *what* tools to use *when*, and *how* to use them effectively. If you end up writing a long-winded e-mail, or prattling on and on over the phone until you bore the other person to tears, or becoming so tongue-tied when leaving a message on voice mail that your recipient has no idea what you're talking about, then all the technology in the world won't help you. The result will still be a "failure to communicate."

The Importance of Listening

When you're trying to communicate, whether one on one or in a group setting, the skill of *listening to others* is just as important as your ability to express yourself. Besides paying close attention to what the other person is saying, *make it clear that you're listening carefully* by looking directly at the person who is speaking. Don't interrupt until that person is done making his or her point. Then respond by asking questions and offering observations based on what was said. Make a habit of listening effectively, and you'll find that your relationships will flower.

The Three Rules of Effective Communication

No matter which tool you're using, you can always be sure of getting your point across powerfully and effectively as long as you keep in mind the following three rules of successful communication:

> ➤ CLARITY—Be *clear* in your writing and speaking. The best way to check the clarity of your writing is to read it aloud, either to yourself or to an obliging friend or family member. It's amazing how quickly you can spot muddy or awkward writing once you hear the words in spoken form.

> ➤ COHERENCE—Is there a *coherent flow* to your thoughts or argument? Do you proceed logically from A to B to C, making a case that your reader or listener can easily follow?

> ➤ BREVITY—"When in doubt, throw it out!" This admonition not only applies to your refrigerator, but to your writing as well. Whatever you want to say, your message will come across much more forcefully when your communication is *concise* and *to the point*.

Mastering the Telephone

I love the telephone. I can think of no item in our lives that is more important on a daily basis, and none that is used more inappropriately by more people.

SURVEY SAYS

What Women Really Think About Men's
Lack of Communication Skills

"Men say things without thinking."

"They don't call their girlfriends for special occasions."

"Men tend to interrupt when someone else is talking."

"They're insensitive in conversation."

"They ignore or laugh off serious discussions."

"They speak before they think."

"They talk in a condescending way."

Bottom line: we have become slaves to the phone, rather than masters of it.

A case in point: I was talking to my sister just the other day in our offices, when the phone rang. She answered as usual, "Hello, this is the Emily Post Institute . . . Yes . . . uh-huh . . . I see . . ."

And on it went. I could see the writing on the wall, and so I left her office to get some work done. Even though our conversation was literally in mid-sentence, the ringing phone meant our conversation was doomed to be interrupted. When she *continued* to talk to the person on the phone, I knew our conversation was finished for good.

I don't mean to pick on my sister; I'm just as guilty of this sort of phone behavior, and, in my experience, so are we all. For some reason, as a society we have conferred on phone callers the unique right to interrupt us at any time, no matter what we're doing. Worse yet, the phone conversation has taken precedence over the in-person conversation. Want to talk to the person in the next office, but he's busy with someone else? No way could you walk in and usurp his time for ten minutes. But call him on the phone and you can talk away, no problem.

This attitude of phone supremacy is just plain wrong—and we can change it, one person at a time. Here are two modest proposals for regaining mastery over the telephone:

Etiquette Imperative

....

The person who is with you takes precedence over the person who is calling you on the phone.

....

1. When you're talking in person with someone and the phone rings, *don't answer it.* Let your answering machine or voice mail pick up the message.

2. If you feel you must answer the phone, *tell the caller that you'll ring them back later, then end the conversation.* Then be sure to call back as soon as you can.

This advice holds even more true for cell phones, which have spread the scourge of phone supremacy to every part of daily life. For example, one day I was shopping for a specific type of drill. The salesman was talking to another customer. After a few minutes they finished their conversation, and he turned to me. I had just started explaining what I was looking for when his cell phone rang. Cutting me off in mid-sentence, the salesman reached for the phone and answered it. It was a customer. As he talked and talked and talked, for nearly ten minutes, I got more and more angry. Here I was, a live body, standing right in front of him, after patiently waiting my turn. And now, just because someone called him on his cell phone, that person had precedence over me.

So I stood there cooling my heels, and when he was finally done I asked him why he interrupted our conversation to take the call, making me wait.

"Hey, I got a call. I had to talk to the person," he replied, as if the answer were obvious. I left without the drill.

In retrospect, I made one mistake in this encounter. I should have gone to see a store manager and file a complaint. I was never going to win an argument with that salesperson, but the store manager should be aware of his employees' behavior. Compound that salesperson's attitude by the thousands of salespeople employed by that company nationwide

Tips for Taking Control of Your Phone

➢ Be sure you have an answering machine or voice mail system—then let it do its work if the phone rings while you're in the middle of a conversation.

➢ If possible, turn off your phone's ringer whenever you're talking with someone in person—or at least set the phone on vibrate/silent ring mode.

➢ If you're having a phone conversation and another call comes in on your "call waiting," the same advice holds. Either ignore the incoming call and let your voice mail pick up, or break away briefly from your initial conversation with an apology, take the new caller's name and number, and call them back when your first call is done.

➢ When it comes to "call waiting," the one absolute no-no is to end your conversation with your first phone mate in order to take the new call. This should never be done, short of an outright emergency or a highly unusual circumstance (like receiving a call from Australia or from your ninety-year-old great-grandmother). Your first conversation takes precedence; your attention belongs to that person, and no one else.

and the company stands to lose a lot of business. By instituting a policy that in-person conversations take precedence over phone calls, they would not only improve their customer relations but would also be taking one more step toward breaking the telephone's hold over the human race.

Volume Control

People in the waiting areas of airports have heard it; train, bus, and plane passengers know it even better; and for office colleagues in adjoining cubicles, it's a painful fact of daily life.

I'm talking about the telephone voice. *You* know the voice I mean— that booming, oblivious-to-the-world tone that everyone seems to adopt as soon as they pick up a telephone receiver.

In fact, there's a good reason for our tendency to talk loudly on the phone. When communicating on the phone, we aren't being supplied with the visual clues we would normally have when talking with someone in person. As a result, we compensate by speaking in a louder voice. This habit may also have a historical component: when phones were first invented, people *had* to shout to be heard on the other end. Technology has solved that problem, but people don't seem to have caught up with this new reality. This is especially true if the other person's voice sounds somewhat distant. We automatically assume that we need to speak up to be heard, as well.

Bottom line: talk at your normal voice level, unless the person on the other end of the line asks you to speak louder. In most cases, an ordinary conversational tone works just fine.

The Cell Phone

The cell phone is a decidedly mixed blessing. It's a wonderfully convenient way to communicate—but if a cell isn't used with consideration for the people around you, it also can make life miserable for everyone within earshot.

Fifteen years ago when my wife and I went out to the movies, we would tell the sitter where we would be. There was no number where we could be reached, other than calling the theater itself in the case of dire emergency. Nowadays, during seminars I tell the audience that the proper course of action is to turn off their phones when sitting in a movie theater. As sure as the sun will rise tomorrow, someone will raise their hand to ask, "What if my baby-sitter needs to reach me? I *need* to leave the phone on in case there's a problem."

"You have two options," I answer. "Option one: turn off the phone. Then, at the end of the movie, check for messages and call home if you need to. Option two: put your phone on vibrate mode; then if it shimmies, get up, go out to the lobby, and answer it. Under *no* circumstances is it acceptable to leave it on ring mode, or to answer the phone inside the theater. End of story."

The "Unnecessary Call" Syndrome

I remember the first time I saw this phenomenon in action. Back in the mid-'90s, we were visiting our daughter at school on Parents' Day. As we were strolling between buildings to the next class, a woman walking in front of us took out her cell phone and made a call. She was using her "phone voice," so naturally we heard every word as clear as a bell.

"Hi, honey . . . You're in the classroom? I'm on the sidewalk outside the building. I'll be there in just a minute. Bye!"

Now, *that* was an important call if ever I heard one. I couldn't help wonder: When the husband's phone rang in the classroom, did it disturb the other people there? Undoubtedly it did—at least to the extent that everyone in the classroom had to check to see if it was *their* phone that was ringing.

Bottom line: just because you've got a cell phone doesn't mean you *have* to use it.

The "I'm Totally Clueless" Syndrome

Once, as I was waiting to board a plane, a woman standing in line spoke on her phone to a friend the entire time. On and on she went, about how she would be arriving soon, and how they would be going out to dinner that night. Everybody in the jetway was forced to listen to the conversation—but she clearly had *no idea* she was subjecting us to her conversation.

The capper was when she began asking her friend where they should go to eat that night. They couldn't decide. Suddenly a hand reached out and tapped the lady on the shoulder. "I can suggest a good restaurant for you if it will help," the man belonging to the hand offered. She looked around, horrified—then quickly ended the conversation.

Everyone got a chuckle out of the situation—but unfortunately, not all examples of the "totally clueless syndrome" are as benign as this one. Instead of simply talking about where to eat, some people hold public discussions involving incredibly personal or confidential information. I've had people tell me they've overheard intimate details about peoples' love lives or a family member's life-threatening illness, or the vivid specifics of the most lurid gossip.

Bottom line: if you must make a call in a public place like an airport, restaurant, or theater, excuse yourself, go to the lobby, the rest room, or outside—then make the call where it won't disturb the people around you, and where your private conversation will remain that way. And if you *must* make or receive a call while you're riding public transportation, keep it as short and low-volume as possible.

Lodging Cell Phone Complaints

One hopeful note is that commuters are starting to rebel against cell phone users who insist on talking on a railway car or bus. Amtrak has instituted a "quiet" car on many of its most traveled routes—a car that allows no cell phones, pagers, computers, or any other device that might disturb the other riders.

If someone's cell phone use on a public conveyance is disturbing you, make your complaint to management—in this case, the conductor. It is then incumbent on management to enforce the rules.

In restaurants, if someone is talking on a cell phone and it's bothering the people at your table, talk to the waiter or maître d'. Have him or her address the issue with the offender. The same rule of thumb holds if you're at a movie theater, concert, or play: Talk to an usher or see the manager, and never try to approach the offender directly.

E-mail Hell

E-mails are public documents. Period.

The absolute bottom line: *if you can't post what you have to say in an e-mail on a bulletin board, then don't send it.*

A young married woman sent her husband an e-mail, recounting the pleasures of their preceding night in some detail. It was an innocent and romantic gesture. Unfortunately for her, he wasn't the only one to read it. The e-mail went public somehow—the how doesn't matter—and before she knew it, 15 million people around the world knew the full story of her romp with her husband, all because she broke the cardinal rule of e-correspondence: *e-mails are public documents.*

Speed Kills

The speed we love about e-mail is also an insidious danger.

Here's the situation: you receive a nasty e-mail. Hopping mad, you decide to respond immediately. The words flow quickly, until finally you hit that last exclamation mark and, with great satisfaction, punch the "send" button.

"That'll show him," you think to yourself. Five minutes later, feeling much calmer now, you reread your sent mail—and realize that it was way over the top. Unfortunately, there may be no way to retrieve it. Once you hit that "send" button, your missile rockets out of your server and can never be recalled.

The problem with any immediate response is that it invariably will be much more about your anger than about solving the problem at hand. When penning any sort of message, *take your time.*

Bottom line: once you're done composing an e-mail, never simply press the "send" button. Always choose "send later," or "draft," or whatever option on your e-mail program will allow you to pause, review, and reflect on that missile before it takes off. After a little time has gone by, go back and reread your message, make any edits you think it needs, and *then* send it off.

You Are What You Write—Warts and All

Whenever you send a written communication, whether by regular mail or e-mail, your writing style will be on full view, warts and all. Typos, misspellings, malapropisms, grammatical errors—they all stand out. These mistakes reflect on *you,* so make a point of carefully reviewing everything you write, even informal notes. If you send your boss an e-mail containing misspelled words, your boss is likely to focus on *and remember* those misspellings—and the content you worked so hard on will be compromised as a result.

7

Meeting and Greeting

HAVE YOU EVER WATCHED the TV game show *Wheel of Fortune*? One night I watched the usual celebration unfold at the end of the show, with the relatives rushing down to congratulate the lucky winner. This time, however, when Pat Sajak, the host, held his hand out to the winner to offer his congratulations, the winner chose that moment to abruptly turn away from Pat and kiss his wife. Pat stood there looking down at his empty hand, then looked up at the camera with a "what do I do now?" look on his face. Finally he shrugged his shoulders, retracted his hand, and waved to the audience.

In front of thousands of viewers, he gave a perfect demonstration of what happens when people don't do what's expected. When people know the appropriate manners for a given situation and use them, everything's great and we all move on. When they don't, as in the Pat Sajak incident, that's when confusion and hurt feelings can arise.

This is never more true than when meeting and greeting other people. Whether you're greeting relatives, friends, acquaintances, or new faces, starting out on the right foot is so much easier than having to recover from an introductory faux pas. If you use thoughtful manners to smooth the way, chances are the rest of the occasion—not to mention ensuing encounters—will go smoothly and comfortably as well.

Greeting People

There are four simple steps that are guaranteed to make people think highly of you from the moment you first greet them. Here they are:

1. **STAND UP.** This is *always* the start of a good greeting, whether you're a man or a woman. By standing up, you engage the person you are greeting on an equal level—eye to eye. Remaining seated, on the other hand, sends the signal that you think you're more important than the other person, and don't need to stand—not the message you want to convey at the start of an interaction, to say the least. If you're seated in a place where getting up is awkward, make a clear attempt to rise and apologize briefly as you greet the other person: "It's a pleasure to meet you, John. Please excuse me—it's a little cramped in here."

2. **SMILE AND MAKE EYE CONTACT.** A smile indicates warmth, openness, and a genuine interest in the person you are greeting. Making eye contact is also critical. Looking into a person's eyes shows that you are focused on and interested in that person. Doing the opposite, on the other hand—looking away as you greet someone—will make you appear aloof, disinterested, or rude.

3. **STATE YOUR GREETING CLEARLY.** If you are the person who is initiating the greeting, your opening should be along these lines: "Hello, my name is Tom Meyers." If you are on the receiving end of the greeting, your response should be something like: "Hi Tom, I'm Jerry Smith. I'm pleased to meet you." If there are others in your group, you might add, "This is Cindy White and Jim Jones. Please join us. We were just talking about . . ." The key is to offer or acknowledge the spoken greeting, then invite the person joining the group into the conversation.

4. **SHAKE HANDS.** For more information on the all-important handshake, read on.

The All-Important Handshake

The handshake is a seminal moment in a greeting—a moment when touch is as important as sight, smell, and hearing. The right handshake makes everything flow smoothly. The wrong handshake turns the focus on the error.

There are three types of handshakes—only one of which is acceptable:

> ➤ **WRONG: THE BONE CRUSHER HANDSHAKE**—Handshaking should not be a macho contest, and it should *never* leave the other person in pain or discomfort.

> ➤ **WRONG: THE LIMP-WRIST HANDSHAKE**—This handshake feels like you're gripping wet noodles. It conveys neither warmth nor interest.

> ➤ **RIGHT: THE FIRM HANDSHAKE**—As the spoken greeting occurs, the person initiating the greeting should reach forward with his right hand, palm facing to the left, and the person receiving the greeting should reciprocate. Grip firmly and warmly, without squeezing hard. Two or three pumps are all that's needed—so don't prolong the event by holding on longer than is necessary.

The Man-Woman Issue

Historically, men were not expected to shake hands with women. Today, as part of meeting and greeting, everyone is expected to shake hands with everybody.

Emily Post on Shaking Hands

In her original etiquette book, Emily Post described the errors of poor handshaking styles this way:

A handshake often creates a feeling of liking or of irritation between two strangers. Who does not dislike a "boneless" hand extended as though it were a spray of seaweed, or a miniature boiled pudding? It is equally annoying to have one's hand clutched aloft in grotesque affectation and shaken violently sideways as though it were being used to clean a spot out of the atmosphere. What woman does not wince at the viselike grasp that cuts her rings into her flesh and temporarily paralyzes every finger?

Making Introductions

There you are, talking with someone cute and interesting you've just met at a cocktail party, when suddenly your great-aunt Winifred (I actually *had* a great-aunt Winifred) approaches. Instant panic: you want to make the introduction correctly, but several problems immediately rear their ugly heads: Who do you introduce to whom, how do you do it, and what exactly *was* Cute-and-interesting's name, again?

WHO DO YOU INTRODUCE TO WHOM? Okay—let's take a deep breath and start at the beginning: entire books have been written describing all the different permutations of who you should introduce to whom first. In fact, the technical rules are so complicated, you'll need a protocol officer at your side at every social event you attend if you want to go by the book. My advice is: fire the protocol officer and trash the book, because this one is easy. *Just talk to the more important person and introduce the other person to the more important person.*

> **CORRECT:** "Mr. Important Person, I would like to introduce Mr. Other Person to you."

> **INCORRECT:** "Mr. Important Person, I would like to introduce you to Mr. Other Person."

When Winifred approaches, first make the decision that she is the more important person in this encounter and say, "Aunt Winifred, how nice to see you!" (Kiss, kiss on the cheeks.) "Please, let me introduce Cute-and-interesting to you." (I'll deal with the problem of remembering her name in just a minute.) Next, turn to Cute-and-interesting and say,

So Who's More Important?

When you make an introduction, the rule says first talk to the more important person:

A client or prospect is more important than your CEO.

An older person is generally more important than a younger person.

If it's a man and a woman and all else is relatively equal, make her the more important person.

"Cute-and-interesting, this is Mrs. Post, my great-aunt Winifred. I'm so pleased to introduce you." Then turn back to Aunt Winnie and continue, "Aunt Winnie, we were talking about how cold the weather is. You just came up from Florida. How was it there?" And off you go . . .

Remembering Names (or Not)

We all forget names. I haven't met anyone who hasn't, at one time or another, been in the awkward situation of having to make an introduction when they were unable to remember one of the people's names.

So what do these folks do?

Usually—nothing. That's right: nada. Zip. No introduction. Let them introduce themselves, goes the thinking, and get me out of the pickle I'm in.

Well, that might work in the short run. But I guarantee you that the people whom you failed to introduce will not think very highly of you for making *your* problem into *their* problem. And I don't blame them one bit.

Okay, so what *should* you do?

Admit your problem, and ask for help. Here's how it works. Let's say you've started the introduction. "Aunt Winifred! How nice to see you." (Kiss, kiss on the cheeks.) "Please, let me introduce . . ."

At this point, you stop and turn to Cute-and-interesting with an apologetic smile and say, "I am so embarrassed—I can't remember your name." Now, Cute-and-interesting could leave you hanging by not saying anything, but in all my forgetful years I've never seen this happen. Most likely, she'll reach out her hand to Aunt Winnie and say, "Hi, I'm Carmen Sanobel. It's so nice to meet you, Mrs. Post."

You say to Carmen (with heartfelt gratitude), "Thank you, Carmen" (thus imprinting her name on your forgetful brain). Then you turn to Aunt Winnie and continue, "Aunt Winnie, we were talking about how cold the weather is. You just came up from Florida. How was it there?" And off you go . . .

We've all been there, and we all know how it feels. The important thing is you were able to make the introduction. Carmen and Winnie are going to blow right past your small stumble, because you did the important thing: you acknowledged them both and made it possible for them to start having a positive interaction—which is *much* more important than remembering Carmen's name.

On the other hand, you'd better make sure you imprint Carmen's name permanently on your memory from now on if you hope to see her in the future. It would be in *extremely* poor taste to have your great-aunt Evie (yes, I had a great-aunt Evie, too—*and* a great-aunt Florence) come over and have to ask Carmen for her name once again.

Some tips on remembering the names of people you meet:

Focus. I know it can be hard, especially if she's gorgeous and you're quaking in your boots as you try not to do or say something incredibly stupid. But no matter how hard it may seem, you've got to forget her looks for one moment and focus instead on her face and on the words you are hearing.

"Tom, I'd like to introduce Gorgeous to you," your great-aunt Florence says.

What you *don't* do is mumble, "Nice to meet you." Instead, say with a clear voice, "Gorgeous, what a pleasure it is to meet you!" And as she replies, you repeat to yourself, "Gorgeous, Gorgeous, Gorgeous." Then make a point of saying her name out loud at various points during the conversation that follows. The goal is simple: *imprint that name.*

Use Imaging. Another time-honored trick is to immediately picture some image or idea that you associate with the person's name. For example, you might think to yourself, "Gorgeous—like in *Drop Dead Gorgeous,* the movie." This sort of association actually increases the amount of neural connections devoted to a particular memory, providing an automatic (and very effective) hint every time you find it necessary to recall your newfound friend's name.

It's All About Being Comfortable

In summary, the rules of a gracious greeting are simple:

➢ Stand

➢ Smile and look 'em in the eye

➢ Say a pleasant greeting

➢ Offer a firm handshake

➢ When introducing people, talk to the more important person first

Remember, your overriding goal is *to be comfortable* with the people you are meeting, and *have them be comfortable* with you. When we are

"Nice to Meet You, Too."

It's happened to all of us: you approach a stranger at a dinner party, politely extend your hand, and say, "Hi, my name is Bill Owens."

The stranger extends his hand in turn and says, "Nice to meet you."

And that's all. No name.

This is one of the most vexing "meet and greet" problems I've come across. Bill is left hanging, thinking to himself, "Hey, stranger. Have you got a name? What's the deal here?" Meanwhile, the stranger forges onward, doomed to repeat his transgression wherever he goes.

Bottom line: don't be like the stranger—unless you want to leave a poor first impression that you may never recover from.

uncomfortable, we tend to focus on our discomfort, rather than giving the situation the opportunity to grow. When we are comfortable with each other, we can move forward together in a positive way.

Mr. and Mrs. or John and Mary?

The real issue in the debate about using first names as opposed to a more honorific title like "Mr." or "Mrs." is that everybody needs to be comfortable. For that reason, if you're with people who are older than you, or in a formal situation with people you don't know well, always start by using the more formal type of address. If the other person then offers you the opportunity to address him or her differently, politely thank them and proceed.

8

Tipping 101

A H, THE DILEMMAS OF tipping: Should you? If so, how much—and when?

There was a time when you tipped to show your appreciation for good service. Nowadays many establishments, particularly restaurants, automatically figure in potential tips when deciding what to pay their workers. This allows the restaurant to pay lower wages—and turns tips into an absolute necessity for those workers. In these cases, the only way to show special appreciation is to tip *more* than the expected amount.

With other professions, such as furniture movers, the old concept still holds: they are getting paid a good salary to do their job, and any tip you give is considered an expression of thanks for outstanding service. The same goes for any business that posts a tip jar on the counter; in these cases a tip is not necessary, and whether you decide to leave one or not is totally up to you.

On the other hand, if you fail to tip when it's expected, you can be assured that the gesture will be perceived as being unfriendly—a message you probably don't want to send. Even in cases where the service is truly bad—for example, when your restaurant waiter is inattentive or rude—the wrong response is to leave a greatly reduced tip. This won't accomplish anything other than annoying your server. If there is a real problem with someone's service, leave a tip that's on the *low end of usual*—then make a point of taking up your complaint with that person's manager or supervisor.

Appropriate Tips for Business and Professional Services

Barbers

Tip 15 to 20 percent of the bill, but never less than a dollar. If you are in a fancy salon in which different people provide hair washing, shaving, and so on, give a tip of one or two dollars to each service provider and a tip equal to 15 to 20 percent of the bill to the person who cuts your hair. When the owner cuts your hair, you don't need to leave a tip. But a gift at the holidays is considered a nice gesture.

Deliveries

A supermarket delivery person should receive around two dollars per delivery.

Food deliverers usually get a tip equal to 10 percent of the bill. The tip should be at least a dollar for a small five- to ten-dollar pizza order, and at least three dollars if the order is larger.

Movers

The head mover gets twenty-five to fifty dollars and crew members should receive fifteen to thirty dollars each, depending on the amount of furniture moved. The tip may increase if they also packed your belongings.

Garage Attendants

Give a tip of a dollar to the parking lot attendant who brings you your car when you pick it up. If you keep your car in a garage, you may want to tip the attendants five dollars periodically to ensure prompt service; then offer a larger tip at the holidays.

Trash Collection

Hand out a tip of ten to fifteen dollars per crew member at the holidays. If your service is municipal, check to be sure there is no regulation preventing gifts to crew members before offering them.

Lawn Care

If there's one person who takes care of your place regularly, you should offer him or her a fifteen- to twenty-five-dollar tip at the end of the season.

Grocery Loaders

Tip a dollar if the loader helps you to your car with a normal number of bags and a dollar-fifty to three dollars if you have a large number of bags.

Taxis

Generally, you should tip your driver approximately 15 percent of the cost of the fare—but never less than fifty cents. For a small fare like five dollars it is appropriate to tip 20 percent, or a dollar. In addition, rounding up the tip where appropriate will make life easier for yourself and a little more pleasant for the cab driver. For instance, 15 percent of a twelve-dollar fare comes to a dollar-eighty; in this case, it makes sense to round the tip up to an even two dollars.

Private Cars and Limousines

If you get billed regularly by a car service, the best approach is to ask the company to add a 15 percent gratuity to the bill for you. This way everything is included and you don't have to worry about fumbling for a tip when you arrive at your destination. If you are paying for the trip at the end of the ride, then tip the driver as you would for a taxi.

Sometimes a car service may be provided for you by a company or some other third party. In this case, offer the driver a five-dollar tip at the end of the ride. It's a nice gesture on your part. In Washington, D.C., I once had a car service at my disposal for an entire day. During my downtime between interviews, the driver took me to visit the Vietnam War Memorial, the Korean War Memorial, and several other sites around the Mall. I gave him an extra-large tip as a sign of my gratitude—even though someone else was paying the bill.

Tipping at Restaurants

Coat Room Attendants

Tip the attendant a dollar per coat when you pick up your garments—and two dollars per coat if you've also checked parcels, umbrellas, or hats.

Washroom Attendants

You'll tend to see washroom attendants much more in Europe than in the United States, though there is a recent trend toward having washroom attendants at restaurants in larger U.S. cities. You should tip the attendant no less than fifty cents. If he provides additional service, a proportionately larger tip is in order. Often the washroom will have a plate with some coins on it where you can leave your tip.

Waiters and Waitresses

Generally, a tip equal to 15 percent of the cost of the meal is considered reasonable. If the service is above average, you may want to consider increasing the tip to 20 percent. One important note: the tip is based on the cost of the meal *before* any taxes are added. If the waiter serves the wine or any other drinks, then the cost of these should be figured into the tip as well.

Wait staff at a buffet should be left a 10 percent tip, rather than 15 percent.

Generally, bus staff are not tipped.

Maître d'

Usually, you do not tip the restaurant maître d' or the host or hostess. The harsh truth is, tipping the maître d' is not really likely to get you a good table. On the other hand, if you go to a certain restaurant often, you may want to tip the maître d', host, or hostess five dollars every once in a while to acknowledge their ongoing service and attention to your needs.

Wine Steward

If the restaurant has a wine steward who helps you select the wine and pours it for you, you should tip him or her 15 percent of the wine bill. I'm often asked the question, "What if I buy a four-hundred-dollar bottle of wine? Doesn't it seem a little excessive to tip the wine steward sixty dollars?" My response: if you can handle buying the four-hundred-dollar bottle of wine, then you can handle a sixty-dollar tip for the wine steward. If the wine steward is very attentive and works with you to review the list and identify exactly the right wines to go with your meal, you may even want to increase the tip to 20 percent.

Wine stewards are always tipped in cash. You may choose to tip after the last bottle of wine has been poured. Otherwise, they should and will make themselves available to you as you are getting ready to leave. If they don't happen to be Johnny-on-the-spot at meal's end, *don't* look at the situation as an opportunity to sneak out. Ask the waiter or maître d' to find the wine steward for you.

Bartender

Generally, bartenders are tipped 15 percent of the bar bill. If you're at a restaurant and have drinks while you're waiting for your table, you should leave a 15 percent tip for the bartender before being shown to your table. Remember: if you do tip the bartender and the drinks are part of your total bill, mentally deduct the bar tab from the bill before figuring the tip.

Musicians

There are usually two kinds of musicians in restaurants—those who play in the background, and musicians who go from table to table like traveling minstrels. Musicians who play in the background, such as piano players, will usually have a brandy snifter or some other container to place tips in. As with all tip jars, the decision to tip in this case is entirely up to you. Musicians who travel from table to table should be tipped a dollar when they visit your table plus a dollar for each request. Don't feel you have to wait for the musician to finish playing before tucking into your meal. You are there to enjoy your food, so feel free to eat while you're being serenaded.

Valet Parking

It's appropriate to tip the parking attendant one to two dollars when he or she brings you your car.

Holiday Tipping

Newspaper Delivery

You should give a tip of five to fifteen dollars at the holidays if your paper is delivered by a neighborhood youth. A somewhat larger tip is appropriate for adults who perform this job in the inner city or on rural routes.

Household Help

A cleaning person or a regular baby-sitter should generally be offered a monetary gift of fifteen to twenty-five dollars, plus a small gift. For a baby-sitter, the gift can be from the child(ren).

Residential Building Employees

Superintendents should typically be given a tip of around fifty dollars if they help with deliveries, fix things, or carry heavy items for you— ranging down to twenty dollars or less if these services are not provided.

Doorman

Give a holiday tip of thirty-five to fifty dollars for very helpful door-men, and less for those you don't interact with regularly.

Elevator Operator

A ten- to twenty-dollar tip at the holiday season is an appropriate thank-you for service provided throughout the year. If he or she does something special for you, tip at the time the service is given.

Tipping When Traveling

I'm most uncomfortable about tipping when I'm simply unsure of how much to leave. This issue comes up most often when I'm in countries other than the United States. I want to tip reasonably for the expectations of the country I'm visiting, but I simply don't know what those expectations are.

If you're traveling abroad, take the time to check online or read a good travel book on the region you're heading to—the good ones almost always include advice on tipping. The key is to pin down this information *before* you leave home, so you'll know what's customary once you reach the place you are visiting.

On a Ship

Cruise ships will generally provide a detailed gratuity schedule. Check with your cruise company regarding this schedule before setting sail—then follow it.

At the Airport

Skycaps should be tipped a dollar per bag. Airline ground personnel and flight attendants are not tipped.

Motels and Hotels

Bellman: If he or she helps you with your baggage, tip a dollar per bag, but not less than two dollars in any case. Any additional services, such as bringing you a fax or a package, should be tipped two to three dollars each time.

Doorman: If he or she helps you with your baggage, again tip a dollar per bag but not less than two dollars in any case. If the doorman gets a cab for you, a tip of one to three dollars is appropriate, depending on the weather and how hard he or she had to work to get the cab.

Room Service: Tip 15 percent of the bill, but never less than two dollars. Note that this is *in addition* to the hotel's fee for providing room service. The only exception to this is if the hotel has already added both a room service fee *and* a gratuity on the room-service receipt.

Concierge: Generally, the concierge should be tipped five dollars for arranging your reservation, and so on. You can increase this amount if he or she has gone above and beyond the call of normal service.

9

··

Working Out, or,
Lost in Your Own Thoughts

WHEN MEN ARE WORKING out, they tend to get lost in their own
thoughts. More than once, I've waited for a circuit machine to free
up, only to watch Mr. Oblivious finish with a set and just sit there, holding
the machine. He could easily have alternated sets with me—but he simply wasn't aware of what was happening around him, or he just didn't
care. In either case, he failed to realize the reality that in a public setting
like a fitness center, *you aren't alone*. You're in a group setting that requires
being aware at all times of how your actions affect others. Here are some
of the most common fitness club flubs that men make:

Impressing

If you're trying to look good in order to impress a certain special someone, the best way to do this is with your mind, not your body. Nod and
say hello—then focus on your exercise routine. That's what you're here
for, and even more important, that's what *she's* here for. Believe me, she'll
be far more impressed with how you *act* than how you *look*.

Leaving a Pool of Sweat

Would you want to use a fork that hadn't been washed? The same goes at the fitness center. Let's say Mr. Buff is really pushing his physical limits on an exercise bike. Finally the session ends, and he steps off the bike, still totally focused on his effort, and walks away. Behind him, the handles glisten with his manly perspiration, and the seat has a small pool of sweat on it, waiting for the next lucky exerciser to climb on—maybe even that certain someone he's been trying to impress.

It's not that Mr. Buff refused to clean the machine on purpose—he just didn't think of it. His mind was far, far away, in an endorphin haze. Which brings us back to the central premise of fitness club etiquette: *be conscious of the people around you.*

Imagine this scenario instead: when Mr. Buff steps off, he turns to the next person and says cheerfully, "Just a second—let me clean this off for you." He gives the bike a quick spray with a handy bottle of cleanser, then wipes it dry. This is called being considerate. It's also a great way to make the *right* kind of impression on your fellow club member.

The Unwanted Stare

This one is a toughie. Those close-fitting sports bras and shorts don't always leave much to the imagination. And then there's all that uncovered skin—sometimes lots of it—not to mention the occasional tattoo.

Somehow I've always thought of a tattoo as an invitation to look: after all, why else is it there but to be noticed? The other day, for example, a woman on the yoga mat next to mine took off her jacket to reveal what looked like a large tattoo of Matisse's painting *Dance*, one of the great works of modern art, on her back. I had to consciously work at not staring at her. I would have *loved* to really study that tattoo, but I limited myself to a few discreet looks when her back was turned toward me.

The point is, there's a difference between a look and a stare. Here's the distinction: when you look around you as you work out, your gaze falls naturally on another person, but your focus is on what you're doing. When you stare, you focus on the object of your staring, rather than on what you are doing.

The bottom line: women *know* when you're staring at them, especially

SURVEY SAYS
What Women *Really* Think About Macho Men
....

Here's what the women in our Post Survey had to say about men who are fitness club showoffs:

"Acts like an idiot trying to impress attractive women."

"Acts like Rambo when he's really one of the Three Stooges."

"Admires himself excessively in the surrounding mirrors."

"Flexes constantly."

"Grunts and groans excessively."

"Lift more weight than they can handle."

"Shows off his form in a spandex suit when he's overweight."

"Tries to act buff when he's not."
....

when you're staring at their breasts ("and I have normal-sized breasts," fumed one Post Survey respondent). *They don't like it.* Do you want to impress a woman? Then look, don't stare. You'll impress her most by showing that you're a man who knows how to respect a woman, tattooed or otherwise.

The "I'm More Important Than You Are" Syndrome

I was on a cruise ship recently where the line of jogging machines all face out the top deck windows, providing a fabulous view of the ocean as you work out. The sign-up system for these machines was pretty strict, I was told, for a good reason: it seems a woman had overstayed her time limit on one of the machines a while back, and the guy waiting took a swing at her when she didn't get off. Of course, she didn't help matters by refusing to get off the machine when her time was up. Both transgressors were guilty of the all-too-prevalent "I'm More Important Than You Are" syndrome, which seems to be an occupational hazard of working out.

The best way to deal with difficult people, and to avoid getting labeled as one yourself, is to respect the fitness center's rules:

➤ Follow the schedules for all machines: start on time and end on time. Remember, everyone's there to work out, and everyone has paid for that privilege.

➤ Don't monopolize the machines. Don't use them as spare seats, and don't stand around them talking with your buddies.

➤ If a conflict does arise—someone won't leave a machine when his or her time is up, or repeatedly refuses to clean up after themselves, or leaves weights scattered all over the place—*don't* take it upon yourself to be the club policeman. Instead, point the problem out to staff and let them take care of it.

➤ In the event that *you're* the culprit, admit your mistake forthrightly and make a conscious effort to change your habits. This is a signal that you need to snap out of that altered mind state and start thinking more about how your actions are affecting others.

Hitting on Women in Mid-Workout

Do you ever read those relationship advice columns in men's magazines? They're full of guidance on how to meet women, and one of the places they often recommend is the fitness center. You've got to wonder if any of these writers have ever actually *been* to a fitness center. I admit the idea sounds great in theory: after all, it's a place where a lot of fit, attractive people are gathered to pursue a common interest. So what exactly *is* the appropriate pickup line when the woman you are interested in is sweating on the Stairmaster or straining to complete one last set of curls?

There isn't one.

Most women do not want some guy in their face, breaking their concentration while they're working out. What they want is to be left alone so they can do their routine.

The bottom line: back off. Do your workout, and let her finish hers. On your way out of the club, *after* you've showered and dressed (and are looking and smelling great), you can try striking up a conversation if the opportunity presents itself. At that point, *she* may even be interested in talking to *you*.

Scratching What Itches

If you have an itch, scratch it—right?

Well, that works for your nose. But the Post Survey found that a great many women can't understand why guys need to scratch and adjust their "privates" so often. As we men know, there's usually a darn good reason: either you have an itch, or your privates shifted into the wrong place and need to be rearranged before starting the next exercise.

The real issue, however, is how to "adjust" yourself in a way that doesn't offend the people around you. For example, the "full frontal adjust" is throwing the whole matter in the face of any woman who happens to be nearby—and she is *not* going to be impressed. Instead, if you need to adjust yourself, turn away discreetly before making the "grab and move." If you do this maneuver properly, no one will even be aware of what you're doing.

"But," you say to me, "I don't even realize I'm doing it."

Then start realizing. If you've got to sneeze, you turn away so you don't spray the people around you, right? The same applies to scratching yourself: being considerate means being conscious of what you're doing—and how it affects the people around you.

Workout Shorts: A Modest Proposal

There's no delicate way to put it: whatever your workout routine consists of—from weight machines to stationary bikes to the contortions of yoga—the wrong kind of shorts will leave you hanging out there for the world to see, even when you're wearing a jock strap. And believe me, your fitness club colleagues will find the view neither stimulating nor impressive.

Recommendation: save the basketball shorts for basketball and the running shorts for running. Fortunately, you can now choose from a variety of great, form-fitting workout pants and shorts made of materials that wick the sweat away from your body. They look great, but because the shorts fit tightly like spandex, there'll be no crotch shots when you're lying, sitting, or bending over.

Conclusion: Courtesy Counts

Finally, many of the women we surveyed also report that a number of men are still falling short on the most basic rudiments of fitness club etiquette. In particular, our respondents complained about men who smell, men who talk too loudly, men who talk too loudly on their cell phones, men who leave messes behind them, men who don't put weights away, men who are just plain rude to those around them, and men who swear.

It seems that, all too often, men's baser instincts are let loose at the fitness center. We tend to focus on ourselves during our workouts—after all, that's why we're there—but by being so self-centered, we risk behaving in a way that we ordinarily wouldn't.

If you see yourself reflected in any of these comments, consider altering your actions. The other people at your fitness center will appreciate the effort.

Call If You Can't Make a Class

Yoga classes are very popular at my fitness club, and there are often more people who want to attend them than there are open slots. These folks get very upset when someone blows off class without calling—with good reason. There are plenty of people on the waiting list who would have jumped at the chance to take that spot, even at six in the morning.

The bottom line: if you can't make a class you've signed up for, call the club well in advance and let them know you won't be there.

10

The Sporting Life:
On the Field and
in the Stands

I'VE SEEN ATHLETICS BRING out the very best and the very worst in people. The satisfaction you feel after a hard-fought tennis match, the thrill of sinking a long putt, or the shared sense of triumph when a local team wins a championship are all examples of how sports can uplift us and bring us closer together. But when athletic enthusiasm veers over the line into unwelcome behavior—when a fan starts screaming at the referee, or a tennis player calls his opponent's close shot out when it's really in, or a golfer spends so much time on the course that he neglects his responsibilities at home—then sports can have the opposite effect: they start to interfere with our ability to get along with people around us.

In the heat of the "athletic moment," we sometimes forget that our behavior, both as participants and spectators, reflects on us in general. The fact is, *what you do and how you act during an athletic contest will influence other people's opinions of you.*

Athletics are competitive: the issues of winning, losing, and competing become emotionally charged—that's part of human nature. The problems start when we get so wrapped up in the moment that we forget that our "on-the-field" behavior can eventually affect careers and relationships "off the field."

I'm talking about more than merely yelling at refs. I'm talking about what happens when we become so consumed with the game that we ignore the people around us. (Sports widows everywhere are cheering right now—can you hear it?) I'm talking about what happens when we become so consumed with winning that we cheat in order to win. I'm talking about what happens when *competition* becomes more important than *people.*

It's Okay to Want to Win

I've always been bothered by the phrase "It's not whether you win or lose that matters, it's how you play the game." This maxim implies that either you can care about winning, or you can care about how you play the game, but you can't care about both.

To which I say, "Bull."

I admit it: I *care* about winning. I enjoy pocketing a bet from my weekly golf game. I like being on the winning side in a tough tennis match. I revel in the University of Vermont's hockey team's victories and suffer with them in defeat (lately I could do with a little less suffering and little more reveling). But I also care about how the game is played. If I'm not "on" this particular week in golf and I play poorly, I may kick myself, or even sign up for a lesson to figure out what the heck has gone wrong. But I don't kick my ball to give it a better lie, or "forget" a couple of shots in the rough. I enjoy winning, *and* I care about how I play the game.

When it comes to striking a balance between winning and stretching the rules, amateur athletes have to be especially careful. Often, winning seems to matter even more at the sandlot or in the backyard, where you're playing for "pride," than it does on the professional playing field.

"That's no touchdown—I touched you back by the sprinkler."

"You did not."

"Did too."

Look out—this could get nasty. You'd think the fate of the world rested on the outcome. What started out as a friendly game can quickly degenerate into an argument or worse, and suddenly a friendship is in ruins.

Etiquette Imperative

....

Play by the rules.

No one likes a whiner or a cheat. On the other hand, I've often heard
people talk admiringly about friends and competitors who play the
game not only by the rules, but also by the spirit of the rules.

....

In this situation, "how you play the game" suddenly becomes very
important. Bottom line: being a good competitor matters. *People respect
people who play by the rules.* Either you were touched or you weren't.
Either the shot was in or it was out. Call the play fairly, accept the other
person's opinion gracefully, and move on.

The Luxury Box

Great! You've been invited to watch a game from a corporate luxury box.
Here are a few things to keep in mind to make the day a complete success:

➤ Before you go, get clear on what you should wear. Ask the person
   who's inviting you or someone who has been there. You want to
   fit in.

➤ Enjoy the game. But keep your excitement on the positive side.
   Cheer, don't jeer. Curb any impulse to berate players or refs. Your
   actions will reflect on you and your company.

➤ Enjoy the amenities of the luxury box. Eat and drink, but do so in
   moderation, especially alcohol. If everyone else eats a hot dog, you
   don't want to be wolfing down six. The same goes for beer or
   drinks. In fact, there is no requirement that says you have to drink
   alcohol at all.

➤ At the end of the game, thank your hosts. Then be sure to write a
   thank-you note and send it in the mail or through the interoffice
   mail the next morning.

Do the Little Things That Matter

DON'T BE LATE. For weekend athletes, time is precious. It's irritating for three men to be left standing on the first tee, wondering if number four is going to make it.

DON'T MISS APPOINTMENTS. There's nothing more frustrating than having three people show up to play doubles tennis at six A.M. If you can't make the scheduled match, it's your job to find a substitute.

BE A RESPONSIBLE BORROWER. Borrow my skis, borrow my surf board, borrow my racquet. No problem. Break my skis, break my surf board, break my racquet? Replace the borrowed piece of equipment with a new one of the same or comparable model. It's that simple.

"Yeah, but the one I borrowed was about to break," you say. "Why should I have to replace it with a new one?" Answer: when you borrow, you become responsible for what you borrow, warts and all. If you don't want the responsibility or if the equipment you want to borrow isn't in the best condition, don't borrow the stuff.

This also goes for your neighbors' tools, or anything else you borrow. Once it's in your possession, you are the caretaker for the item. Lose it or break it? Then replace it or fix it like new. You'll stay good neighbors and good friends.

LEAVE YOUR ATHLETIC VENUE IN BETTER CONDITION THAN YOU FOUND IT. Before you leave the gym after your weekly hoops game, check the area for all your belongings *and* for any garbage you or prior groups may have left behind. When you walk onto the putting green, repair your ball marks (the depression left when your ball first lands on the green) and any others you happen to see. When you finish playing tennis on a clay court, take a few minutes to sweep the court and clean off the lines for the next players.

"Wait a minute," you say. "If the guys before us didn't clean up, why should we?"

Whenever I talk to people about etiquette, they want to know why *they* should be considerate, respectful, and honest when the people around them aren't. The reasons are simple, really. First, we don't do

Cheatin' Charlie—The Scourge of the Course

There's no greater problem in sports than the guy who says to himself, "Cheating is okay, as long as I get away with it." You know who I mean: Cheatin' Charlie always shaves a few strokes off his game—until it's club championship time. Now every stroke counts, and players keep score for each other. Suddenly, Cheatin' Charlie, who's entered some pretty low scores, has to post a ninety-eight. Or maybe he'll quit halfway and post a DNF (Did Not Finish). He'll blame the playing conditions, his playing partners, or anything else he can think of—anything except the *real* cause of his problems: himself.

these things to get anything in return—we do them because we believe in their inherent value. Second, nothing in this world is ever going to change until someone starts the ball rolling. We arrive on time, we pick up after ourselves, and we treat others with consideration, respect, and honesty because it's the right thing to do. Lead by example—others will follow, and we'll all be better off for it.

Friendship vs. Changing the Foursome

Pitiful Paul recently posed the following question: "Every Thursday morning for the past four years we've played tennis with Sam. But lately, Sam's become the weak link. We want to ask Andy to join us instead. How do we tell Sam we don't want him to play with us anymore without hurting his feelings?"

Poor Paul. He and his buddies know that their proposed switch will hurt Slumpin' Sam's feelings, and will probably cost them their friendship with Sam off the court as well. Ditching a regular member of your sporting group for *any* reason is a very dicey thing to do. Ditching him because he isn't quite up to your caliber of play is simply not acceptable.

Etiquette Imperative

In any group that has been playing together regularly,
the members enjoy tenure.

A Friendly Wager

It happens all the time. A little action on the competition just to keep it more interesting.

In our regular foursome we joke that the winners of the two-dollar Nassau are really the losers because the winners buy the round of drinks after the match and that round costs more than the combined twelve-dollar winnings. It's the bragging rights that are important.

Just remember, once you make the bet, you're committed. Do not make a bet you can't cover. And if you lose, pay up, immediately.

If the problem really is severe enough that the other members of the group are willing to forgo any further relationship with Sam, then it's important to inform Sam of the group's decision. Maybe Sam is the cause of the breakup of another member's marriage. Now *that* would rise to the level of a legitimate reason for Sam to get kicked out of the group. The transgression had better be something pretty outrageous, though—because the decision to dump a playing partner, whatever the reason, is likely to cost a friendship.

When Fans Go Too Far

Maybe it has to do with being an anonymous face in the crowd, but some people seem to think that when they're at a sporting event they somehow have the right to ignore the feelings of everyone around them. Take, for instance, the fan who yells at a ref during a ballgame. Incensed at the latest close call, he lets fly with a string of highly uncomplimentary comments at the top of his lungs. I've seen the people around the yeller literally cringe at this sort of diatribe. What I really wonder, though, is what his boss, business associate, or potential client seated nearby is thinking. The next day, when the yeller shows up at their offices to conduct business, can his behavior of the night before be ignored?

"Hey, it's a free country," the yeller may argue. "I'm at a game, and I've paid for the privilege of being here. I can yell at the ref if I want to."

He's right. It *is* a free country. And that boss or business associate or client can choose to do business with whomever he or she wants, for whatever reason.

The Golden Rule of Spectating: Keep It Positive

How do you know where to draw the line when rooting for your favorite team? Simple. You should feel free to shout as much encouragement for your team as you can possibly muster. But when your yelling shifts from being encouraging to derogatory—that's when you've stopped playing a supportive role as a spectator.

Any time you shout encouragement, the players on the field will feed off that energy. On the other hand, if your comments or cheering turn negative and you start berating or putting down the players, coaches, or referees, the effect will not only be counterproductive, but you'll also make people around you (who may or may not agree with you) feel uncomfortable.

Bottom line: cheer all you want, but keep it positive.

Referees Are People, Too

I'd like to leave you with one final thought on spectating: *leave the ref alone!*

One point that's often lost amid all the jeering at sports events is the fact that referees are people, too. Basically, they want to make the right calls just as much as the players, coaches, and fans want them to. Unfortunately, referees are faced with a daunting task. A baseball umpire, for instance, might have to make 150 or more calls in a single game. If the baseball umpire makes three calls that could be considered questionable, that means he's still making 147 good calls. That's a 98 percent success rate. In most jobs, a 98 percent average would be admirable. For the umpire, however, those three questionable calls means he's doomed to be on the receiving end of a torrent of abuse.

It gets even worse. You will also have perfectly sensible players, fans, and coaches who see a call one way while the ref sees it another. The ref is right, but that doesn't stop the fans from grousing about how they would have won if it hadn't been for him. They forget all about their team's missed plays, strikeouts, or blown shots and focus on the one call they claim "cost them the game." It's time for these complainers to grow up. The ref didn't cost them the game—their own team's play did.

11

Parents and Kids

Aᴄᴄᴏʀᴅɪɴɢ ᴛᴏ ᴘᴜʙʟɪᴄ ᴀɢᴇɴᴅᴀ, a research organization based in New York:

➤ Only *9 percent* of Americans report that the kids they see in public act respectfully toward adults.

➤ 84 percent of Americans agree that a major cause of disrespect in our society is the fact that "too many parents are failing to teach respect to our kids."

➤ 75 percent of Americans want parents to teach their kids that "cursing is always wrong."

➤ Only 19 percent of adult Americans claim to "never curse."

These last two points highlight a major contradiction in American attitudes toward children's rude behavior. As adults, we are *all* part of the problem—and the potential solution. It doesn't matter whether you are a parent or not.

Children learn by mimicking adult behavior.

Let me repeat that. *Children learn by mimicking adult behavior.*

Example: you're standing in line at the grocery store with a buddy when a mom and her two kids get in line behind you. You're still hot under the collar from an incident that happened on the drive to the store, and you're not shy about letting your friend know your feelings.

"Crazy bastard," you snarl. "Can you believe how he cut me off? The bleep almost hit me! I should have chased him down and taught him a bleeping lesson."

You are, in a word, oblivious.

Meanwhile, the young children standing a few feet away from you have imprinted the following images in their memories:

1. *A grown man swearing*—which must mean that it's okay to swear, at least if you're really mad.

2. *A grown man threatening an act of road rage*—which must mean that it's okay to chase someone down with your car if you're mad enough, and also that it's okay to do violence to another person if you think there's enough justification.

The bottom line: you don't have to have kids of your own to have an impact on childen.

When it comes to teaching kids to be more respectful and less rude, there is no silver-bullet solution. We *all* need to recognize that how we act will be reflected in the behavior and attitudes of tomorrow's adults. If *every* adult starts making a conscious decision to model considerate, respectful behavior in his or her daily life, kids will start reflecting that behavior. The sooner we do this, the sooner our children's behavioral problems will start to be remedied.

Etiquette Imperative

Be extra careful around children. You are already influencing children every time you're around them by the way you act, speak, and carry yourself.

What Women *Really* Think About Men Helping with the Kids

"Men don't pitch in with the kids unless they're asked to."

"They resent having to watch the kids while you go out."

"They opt out of the discipline process, leaving the woman to be the only parent who disciplines the children."

"They don't think to initiate bedtime routines for kids."

"Men ignore the kids if they're otherwise occupied."

So Now You're a Dad!

On June 12, 1979, Anna, my oldest child, was born. At the time, I had no idea how much my life would change as a result. My wife and I had been married for six years, and now . . . all of a sudden, there were three of us.

Our living situation had altered drastically—but old habits die hard. June is strawberry-picking time in Vermont, and about ten days after our daughter was born, I went berry picking. There happened to be a crop of luscious berries that day, bright red, juicy—the height of perfection. I got carried away and came home with a couple of flats full of berries.

In previous years, this sort of hunter/gatherer action on my part would have been hailed as a feat of initiative. Now, however, with a two-week-old baby in residence, the only reaction my wife had was, "What on earth do you think I am going to do with those strawberries? I don't have time to make jam or put them up."

I learned two lessons that day: first, things had definitely changed, and I had to start recognizing that fact. Second, putting up strawberries and making jam is a *lot* of work.

Sharing the Responsibility

Being the male parent is not simply a matter of taking a larger role in chores around the house in order to take pressure off your mate so she can focus on raising the baby. Being a male parent also means being a part of the child care—and not just in the first few weeks. It means being an equal partner in the care of your childen for the next eighteen years, and then some.

Child care takes a couple of different forms:

> ➤ **SHARING THE LOAD.** This sometimes involves serious sacrifice. For instance, on any given Sunday afternoon, just as Joe Namath was snatching victory from the jaws of certain defeat, the phone rings. My daughter is on the line: "Can you pick me up now?" My wife's making dinner, so I have no choice. As I drive down a winding dirt road to pick my daughter up, I would console myself with the fact that I can watch the highlights on the sports segment of the late-night news.

> ➤ **BEING THE DISCIPLINARIAN.** Dads can't always be fun. Discipline is part of parenting, and for it to work, *both* partners have to participate. The mom can't always be the heavy. She will resent you to no end if you're always the parent who consoles the child. Be willing to be the parent who enforces the law, and support your spouse in her choices when *she's* the enforcer.

> ➤ **GOING TO THEIR EVENTS.** I've heard more primary school Christmas concerts than I care to remember. Each one was important to my daughters, and it was also important that both of their parents were there to share in their performance. Whether your child is the star or a member of the chorus, you make time to attend, you applaud thunderously, and you congratulate her as though it were opening night on Broadway.

> ➤ **TALKING WITH YOUR KIDS.** Take the time to listen to your children. They have wonderful thoughts and an ever-fresh perspective, and talking with them will help bring those thoughts out. When I was a young parent, I could always tell the kids whose parents listened to them. If I was driving them home after a visit, they were the kids who would talk your ear off, even though you were a relatively unfamiliar adult. Those conversations were always a joy, especially compared to driving a kid home whose vocabulary consisted of grunted, monosyllabic responses to my questions.

Do as I Say, Not as I Do

The statistics reveal how much we Americans buy into this maxim: 75 percent of adult Americans want to teach children not to swear. But at the same time, *81 percent of us* acknowledge swearing ourselves at least some of the time. In other words, we admit that we're modeling this behavior even though we want and expect different behavior from our kids.

Learning doesn't work that way. I discovered this when my older daughter was in grade school. She had a teacher who I firmly believed was the perfect example of what's wrong with the "guaranteed job" policies in public education—and one day I voiced my displeasure about her *in front of my daughter.* I remember it so clearly. A short while later, during a discussion about a problem my daughter was having with her teacher, I heard my daughter spout my words back at me. The lightbulb immediately went off in my head: how could I possibly expect her to follow my admonition to "respect her teacher," *when I was teaching her to disrespect that same person?*

Kids do *not* understand "Do as I say, not as I do." They *do* understand "Do as I do."

Time passes so quickly. Before you know it, those little toddlers will be off living on their own. So make the effort to share in the raising of your kids. In the process of raising them, you'll build a stronger relationship with your spouse and give your kids the best possible opportunity to grow up happy and successful.

Spectating at Your Kids' Sports Events

We are so proud of our kids. We want them to do well. We want their team to be the best. And sometimes we get carried away: we see a call that seems to be unfair, and we scream at the ref. We see the coach call our son or daughter out of the game, and we scream at the coach. We see a teammate make a bonehead play, and we scream at the teammate. We see our own son or daughter miss a play they've made hundreds of times in the backyard, and we scream at him or her.

All this screaming *doesn't work.* The referee isn't going to change his call; the coach isn't about to suddenly see things your way, bow to the stands in subservience, and send your kid back in; the teammate isn't going to magically turn into a Golden Gloves candidate. And your son or daughter is now likely to be more focused on your incessant, embarrassing screaming than on his or her own play.

A number of youth leagues now have Spectator Standards, and they're serious about enforcing them. One league requires parents to watch a video and sign a statement promising that they'll adhere to the league's standards of spectator behavior. One infraction, and the offending parent is placed on probation. A second infraction, and they're banned from attending future events.

SURVEY SAYS
Parents Need to Improve Their Behavior

The Post Survey reflected the same problems that other surveys have found: spectators at kids' events are too vocal and disparaging toward coaches, referees, and the young players.

Worst of all, 75 percent of our respondents said they think spectators are too vocal and disparaging toward *their own children.* Something needs to change.

Post Survey respondents also believe overwhelmingly that offending spectators should be warned, and that if the offensive behavior continues, they should be asked to leave the event. Unfortunately, that's a little like closing the barn door after all the cows have escaped. A better idea is for organized sports to institute Spectator Standards of behavior and then scrupulously enforce them.

....

PART TWO

Social Life

12

······································

The Top Three Issues
in Social Life

WHEN IT COMES TO considerate behavior, most people tend to be a bit more on their toes when they're socializing—which is a good thing, because the standards are higher in these situations than when you are relaxing in your living room. And as our Post Survey found, women both *notice* and *care about* how men behave in their social lives.

In fact, the Social Life survey was the most popular of our four surveys, with 1,009 women and 161 men responding. When we asked our respondents which male social behaviors bothered them the most, *lack of manners* topped the list. One out of every four respondents listed men's lousy manners—at the dinner table and elsewhere—as a major problem. The other chief complaints involved men who are disrespectful and inconsiderate, and men who are poorly groomed.

Fortunately, our respondents also had very good things to say about men who excelled in some of these same areas: when we asked them to name things that they *liked* about male behavior, the most frequently cited items were mastery of manners, being caring and affectionate, pitching in, and being appreciative and proud of our significant others despite their possible shortcomings.

Manners Absolutely, Positively Make the Difference in Social Life

Our respondents' complaints about men's social manners included failing to open doors for women, showing up late, swearing, "adjusting" themselves in public, not saying "please" and "thank you," and spitting. But the topic that led the pack was table manners.

Many, if not most, dates and social events include eating. According to our Post Survey, women will be watching. Our respondents report being embarrassed or turned off all too often by men who eat sloppily, noisily, too fast, or who talk with their mouth full.

Men who know how to get food into their mouths inoffensively scored significant points with their dates. The same goes for men who stand both when a woman arrives at a table and when she gets up to leave. Other male behaviors that get high marks include eating at a measured pace, paying the bill for the meal, treating the wait staff pleasantly and respectfully, leaving an appropriate tip—and most important of all, making your significant other feel like an honored dinner guest.

Of course, manners don't stop at the dinner table—a fact that a surprising number of men seem to forget. Amazingly, the ability of men to unashamedly pass gas or burp in public is the second most cited "annoying thing" that men do in social situations. Believe me, fellas—you *can* control these bodily functions. And if you can't, you can always excuse yourself and beat a strategic retreat to the men's room.

The key to social success is not to think of "social etiquette" as a series of traps you can stumble into—but as a terrific opportunity to do things *right*, thus pleasing and impressing those you're with. The most telltale result from the Post Social Life Survey was that although poor manners led the list of negative behaviors, good manners were cited even more often on the positive side. When respondents were asked to describe what men "do well" in social life, they mentioned things like:

➤ Holding coats, elevators, doors, and chairs for women

➤ Carrying packages and heavy items

➤ Being careful to make introductions

➤ Walking beside a woman rather than ahead of her

➤ Offering an arm for support and affection

➤ Saying "please" and "thank you"

➤ Simply "being polite," or "being a gentleman," or "being chivalrous"

These gestures are the mark of a man who is aware and respectful of the people around him. Our survey found that the men who got the best grades on manners from their significant others don't just do *one* of these things right—they instinctively do all of them right, most of the time. It's the cumulative effect of good manners that creates a lasting *positive* impression.

Being Disrespectful and Inconsiderate— Men at Their Worst

When men engage in behaviors like interrupting, ignoring, or acting condescendingly, the women who are with them view them as inconsiderate oafs. If you're with a live-in significant other or a spouse, the result is likely to be a very cold shoulder later in the evening or, worse, a bitter fight. If you're out with a date, there may not be another—and you may find your reputation starting to precede you, as well.

The Ideal Escort: Appreciative and Attentive

Disrespect and inconsideration have a flip side: being appreciative and attentive. According to the Post Survey respondents, men who show appreciation and genuine interest on a consistent basis are the cream of the crop.

If you really want to be an appreciative and attentive escort, good communication skills are vital. At least 90 percent of the positive comments about men in this regard involved issues of communication, such as including others in conversation, listening to what others have to say, and complimenting others on their thoughts, appearance, or actions. When it comes to making other people feel appreciated, these facets of human interaction make all the difference in the world.

Dressing Smart, Smelling Fresh, Looking Good

Ever notice a couple out for dinner or at the movies? The woman is dressed nicely—perhaps she's wearing some tailored pants or neat jeans or a skirt with a sweater or a jacket; and if you got close enough to notice any scent you would probably catch a light whiff of perfume. Then there's the guy with her—turned out in wrinkled jeans or scruffy pants, a T-shirt (probably with some inane slogan on it) or a work shirt that still carries the evidence of that afternoon's chores; his hair's a little unkempt, and his scent is one you'd rather *not* notice. They've *got* to be hitched—because if they weren't, she'd drop him like a hot potato.

In the Post Social Life Survey, poor appearance ranked number three among things that disturb women about men. Once again, the good news is that you can score big points by addressing this issue head on. According to our respondents, women particularly like it when men . . .

> Make a little effort to "put on the dog"

> Know how to dress properly for the occasion

> Dress appropriately, but not ostentatiously

> Dress up for a special occasion without complaining about it

> Take pride in their appearance, without having to be reminded or prodded about it

We are not talking fancy here: we're talking about *voluntarily* dressing and grooming yourself in a way that is appropriate for the occasion. Perhaps the most important comment in the above list was the one about men who "take pride in their appearance." I like this respondent's philosophy. She understands that when you look in the mirror, *you* need to appreciate how you look. When you're able to appreciate your appearance, that's when others are going to say, "He looks sharp." And they'll admire you for it.

Combine good grooming with good manners (which, as I've said, is nothing more than treating people with consideration, respect, and honesty) and a willingness to communicate by listening to, focusing on, and complimenting your companion and others—and you have a foolproof recipe for social success.

13

Dating—Just You and Her

M EN DON'T LIKE IT when they look like they don't know what to
do. And don't think women don't notice it. In fact, when a recent
poll queried women about what was most important in a man, confidence came up as the second most important factor.

When a man is out on a date (and this is equally true whether you're
with your wife or on a first date), doing the little things with confidence
goes a long way toward setting the right mood. When you're doing all
the little things to make your companion feel special, your date can focus
completely on having a great time, rather than on the things you *aren't*
doing.

Just You and Her

Sometimes I think my eyes have a mind all their own. There I am with my
wife; my attention is on her, we're talking and having a great time. And
then it happens. Maybe she walks by or sits at the next table or comes
around a corner or steps out of a cab as we're walking down the street. I
must have pretty good peripheral vision, because I usually notice her. I
try hard not to let my head snap around, but the distraction has already

occurred. If it is a really impressive distraction, I may even take a quick breath, the kind that makes a little sound.

The Post Survey is abundantly clear on this point: when you're out on a date, noticing other women is a real mood killer.

Almost half the women responding to the survey recognize that men are going to look at other women. The real key is that you not let it interfere with your focus on the woman you're with. You really want to let her know by the things you do and (sincerely) say that she is perfect to you—and say and do them often.

> "You look great. I really like that skirt."

> "Every other guy at the party is going be jealous of me tonight."

> Buy her some flowers when it's not an event.

> Cook dinner tonight.

> Hold her hand.

The Importance of Flowers

Every time we go to the supermarket, my wife buys flowers. We live in Vermont, where it's pretty monotone all winter. Late fall and early spring—make that mud season—are colorless, too. Putting flowers in a glass vase on the dining room table is her way of fighting the seasons when things don't grow.

If I bring my wife flowers, I make her day. The problem is, I hardly ever bring her flowers. And hardly ever isn't nearly enough.

If you really want to express love and affection, nothing beats roses. They're great for that someone special in your life. She could be your wife or fiancée, or she could be a girlfriend, or just a friend. Roses are

Roses for My Bride

When my wife and I got married, I arranged to have a florist deliver a bouquet of six roses to my wife five days before our wedding. Four days before the wedding he delivered five roses. You get the idea. On the morning of the wedding he delivered a single rose. It's amazing the effect one rose can have. Be creative.

especially appropriate when you are celebrating an anniversary or an extra-special event. But you don't need to wait for a major occasion—you can simply make one up.

"These are for you. I realized it's been one month since our first date."

Opening Doors

All things being equal, as I approach a door with my wife, I'll step forward ever so slightly, open the door, and hold it for her to enter before me. If I'm carrying a parcel, or if for some reason she is clearly there ahead of me and starts opening the door herself, I don't make a scene by rushing forward and pushing her aside so I can open the door for her. Instead, I accept the effort she is making and say, "Thank you." Other times, when she arrives at a door first and starts opening it, if I can I'll reach behind her and take hold of the edge of the door, discreetly taking over the task of opening it, and then hold it for her so she can enter first.

The Revolving Door Dilemma

Confusion reigns over this issue because it involves conflicting rules: the rule that a woman should go through a door ahead of her companion versus the rule that a man should enter a revolving door first because the door is heavy. Whenever confusion exists, the solution lies in *communication*. The real problems arise when you act indecisively. So be prepared to make a quick decision as you're approaching the door: "This door looks hard to move, so I'll be the gentleman and offer to go through first," or, "Look, the door is already moving, meaning it'll be easy to push—so I'll be the gentleman and suggest that she go first."

Once you've made your split-second decision, immediately communicate your intentions to your companion. "Please go ahead." Or, "Here, let me go first and get it moving for you." Be confident, and act confidently. The situation will resolve itself, and you'll come through looking good.

The Limo

You've planned a very special evening, limo and all, and you want it to get off on the right foot. The limo pulls up to a stop right at the door of the restaurant. This is great! Now, who opens the car door? You don't want to jump out too fast and look unsophisticated in these matters. On the other hand, maybe you'll look helpless, a little less manly, if you let someone else get that door for you, especially if the driver has to run around the car while you wait inside, wondering what to do.

Herein lies the key to almost all the problems with etiquette: uncertainty about what to do. As previously noted, women like men who are confident. Indecision—even about something as trivial as whether or not to open the limo door yourself—can mar the start of this special evening you've worked so hard to arrange.

So here's what you do: wait. And while you're waiting, smile at her. Tell her how great she looks. Take this moment and enjoy it with her. And then, as the driver finally opens the door for you and holds it, you get out first and reach for her hand to help her out.

Helping Her with Her Coat

This one's easy.

Do it. And then take both coats to the coat check and get the claim ticket. When you leave, make sure you leave a tip of a dollar per coat in the tip jar.

Walking Together

The rule of thumb here is that the man always walks on the outside (the side closest to the street). Most of the time this rule works very well. However, it's rare that any rule works all the time, and this one is no exception.

Imagine, for example, that you are walking down the street with your date, holding hands, and it comes time to cross to the other side of the street. As you get to the other side, you realize that you're now on the inside. *Don't* make a show of switching places. In this instance, holding hands and enjoying the moment is more important than switching to the "correct" side.

Another exception is when you have reason to feel that walking on the inside of your companion is appropriate for safety's sake. In this case, by all means do it.

Holding Chairs

I've always believed that one of the most awkward moments at a dinner table occurs when the woman next to you gets up to go to the bathroom. Do you stand?

The Post Survey is clear on this point: women want and expect you to stand up, at least when you are out on the town. So if this is impossible—for example, if you're in a booth—don't worry about it. But all things being equal, stand whenever your companion does.

Whenever you arrive at a table for a non-business meal, offering to hold a chair for your date, the women on either side of you, or the honored guest (if she's female) is a great, gracious thing to do. You may even get an appreciative smile and a "Thanks." Likewise, when rising from the table at the end of the meal—provided you can do it without causing a scene—you should help move your dinner companion's chair away from the table by grasping the back and gently pulling as she starts to push it back in order to stand up. It's a nice gesture on your part.

The one exception: when you're at a business function, the rule of thumb is *not* to hold a chair for anyone, male or female, unless there is a physical need.

Ordering

According to the Post Survey, three out of five women do *not* want men to order a meal for them at a restaurant. So you need to be absolutely sure how the person you are with feels about this issue before going ahead and ordering for her.

The one caveat here is to know the woman you are with: girlfriend, significant other, mother, daughter, grandmother, friend, or business associate. If you are certain she would be honored to have you place an order for her, first ask her what she would like. When the waiter comes to the table, go ahead and make the order for both of you.

This is another case where the rule itself matters not at all. What really matters is the confidence and courtesy you show by knowing how the other person wishes to be treated, and treating her accordingly.

Who Pays?

When it comes to paying the bill at a restaurant, there is a simple rule of thumb: the person who does the inviting pays for the meal. This rule works equally well in the business world and in your social life.

If you do the inviting, expect to pay, and do so without hesitation. If the woman does the inviting and you're uncomfortable having her pay for the meal, talk to her about this when she first extends the invitation. You might offer to "go Dutch," for instance. It's a nice gesture, and if she refuses then you know she was really serious about inviting you *and* picking up the tab.

If she invites you to an event, on the other hand, that leaves an opening for you to make a counter-invitation of your own, such as: "That would be great. I would love to go with you. May I take you to dinner before the concert?"

Finally, when in doubt, communicate. If there is any question in your mind about the subject of who pays, raise the issue early and resolve it promptly. The moment when the check arrives at the table is *not* the time to start asking if you can help pay. By resolving the issue ahead of time, you won't have to worry about it during the dinner. Your companion will be both appreciative of your offer and comfortable in the knowledge that you both understand the situation clearly. You and she can then relax and concentrate on having a wonderful time together—which is what it's all about.

14

....

On the Town

PEOPLE LIKE TO WATCH sitcoms like *I Love Lucy, Seinfeld, Friends,* and *Cheers* because they hit home. By providing a humorous look at the conundrums that arise among groups of friends, these shows allow real people to enjoy the spectacle of fictional characters facing (and working through) difficult and embarrassing situations without any real people getting hurt.

And therein lies the problem for us mortals. Unlike TV's fake "friends," when personal misunderstandings or disagreements crop up in our own social circles, people can feel hurt or embarrassed or disappointed or left out, and our situations don't get resolved in 24 minutes.

In our Post Survey, respondents consistently identified several key "group issues" that are most likely to give rise to discord: choosing a group activity that everyone will enjoy; dividing expenses equitably, especially at a restaurant; having to put up with unnecessary "displays of affection" by a couple that is part of the group; and inconsiderate behavior by individual group members—what I call "small grossnesses," but which can have a big effect on group morale. (Flirting is another problematic "group issue" that made everyone's list—but this subject is so emotionally charged and complex that we've given it a chapter of its own—see chapter 18.)

Public Displays of Affection

Every now and then, as I'm walking down the street, I'll notice a couple wrapped around each other.

"Take it somewhere private," I think to myself. Then I wonder—am I just being a prude? Does it matter where displays of affection occur? Are they okay in one situation, but not another? Where do you draw the line on what's okay and what isn't?

Cut to Rome, Italy. If you ever take a walk along the Tiber River or through the Borghese Gardens on a Sunday afternoon, you're likely to see a lot of couples engaged in hot and heavy kissing. Usually the action is limited to embracing and lip locks—but not always. One Sunday afternoon my wife and I were enjoying a brief stop at the Spanish Steps. We were on a landing about halfway up the stairway, leaning against one of the stone railings. The view was magnificent: hundreds of people were sitting on the steps; below them we could see people strolling arm in arm down the Via Condotti, which stretched into the distance as far as the eye could see.

Then I noticed that the view was pretty magnificent right next to us, too. I nudged my wife. "Look at that," my eyes said to her. The young girl sitting next to us on the stone railing was pretty cute, but that wasn't all I was looking at. Her boyfriend was embracing her passionately, his hands just south of her shoulders, and it *wasn't* a muscle massage he was giving her.

We looked but didn't stare (see chapter 9 for a discussion of this technique), trying hard to mind our own business and enjoy the wonderful vista. But the view to our right proved just too tough to ignore, so reluctantly we departed.

Was it my problem or their problem? I don't know. But I *do* know that if she had been *my* daughter, I wouldn't have been very happy about her behavior. And I'm not alone. Maybe in Europe—or at least in Italy—this type of public display is accepted practice. But according to our Post Survey, as far as folks in the United States are concerned, necking or petting is *not* acceptable unless you're in a relatively private setting.

So if you're out in public or participating in a group activity with your date or significant other, be affectionate and attentive, but keep the smooches short and sweet.

Sharing Expenses

It's great to be the host, or the guy with the car, or the guy with the boat. But sometimes it can be lonely. Especially when it's time to open the wallet and pay for the drinks and munchies or the gas or any other expense.

When it's not your house or your boat or your car, think about the other guy. Offer to chip in and buy a tank of gas or pick up supplies for the next poker game. He may never have asked, but you can be sure he'll appreciate your contribution.

Bar Etiquette

Bars are great places to hang out with your friends or meet new people. The problem is that slips and mistakes, which can be compounded by alcohol, can turn a fun evening into a disaster.

Before you go out, assess the situation you are going to be in. Understand clearly if it is a purely social evening or if it relates to business. I know one man who enjoys going to bars, but he simply never lets loose if he's out with people from work. He knows he's always making an impression on people even when it is completely outside the confines of the office.

Buying a Drink

What a nice gesture. Maybe it's even an opening gambit in getting to know someone new. But be aware that offering to buy a drink is an offer without a quid pro quo. And when you make the offer, she may take you up in spades. Instead of a pleasant mid-priced drink or a glass of wine, she

---

"Loose Lips Sink Ships."

Be very careful about the content of your conversation in a bar. You and your fellow workers or your friends may think your conversation is private, but, in fact, you have no idea how easily the people at the next booth or bar stool may hear what you are saying. Keep work topics at work and private conversations for private places. Use this time as an opportunity to get to know the people from work on a social level, not a business level.

---

may order a cosmopolitan. Once you've made the offer, you're on the hook.

If you do offer to buy a drink, make sure that she sees the bartender make it and that it is delivered to her without any chance of it being "doctored." This is for her safety and yours as well.

Buying Rounds

If a group of people goes out, rather than buying individual drinks, each member of the group may buy a round, in a "this one's on me" mentality. Just be sure that one of the rounds is on you. Nothing annoys people as much as those who don't carry their share of the load.

Alcohol

Going out to a bar with some friends, relaxing, shaking off the stress of a hard day's work—it's all lots of fun as long as it stays fun. Be wary of the dangers of the effects of alcohol, especially as they can make you a little more combative and argumentative and you may not even realize it. Guard against getting into a fight—physical or verbal.

The Etiquette of Splitting the Bill

Consider this dilemma: Donald and his wife, Mary, frequently go out to eat with two other couples. Don and Mary don't drink, while their fellow diners all enjoy a glass or two of fine wine over dinner. What's more, Don has recently changed his dietary habits, and nowadays he often orders a simple soup and salad while everyone else goes for an appetizer and a main course.

When it comes time to pay up, their ritual has been that each couple pulls out a credit card, and the bill is split into three equal parts. Lately, however, Don can't help noticing that he and Mary are invariably subsidizing a fair portion of their friends' meals.

"I'm getting tired of this," Don says to himself. "Our share of last night's bill was eighty dollars, but Mary and I only ordered fifty dollars' worth of food." Don also values his friendships, so he suffers in silence, the pressure inside him slowly increasing, building toward the day when he finally blows. And *that* does promise to be an awkward moment.

If you are one of the Dons of this world, there are two things you can do to remedy the situation. In either case, talk with one or both of the other males before you head out to the restaurant. Don could say, "I'm looking forward to tonight, but I've got one thing I could sure use your help on. Mary and I don't drink and, well, I've cut back on the amount I'm eating, too—trying to do something about this gut. Anyway, with us ordering less, how would you feel . . .

Option #1: . . . "If I ask the waiter or waitress for a separate bill for Mary and me?"

Option #2: . . . "If Mary and I contribute our part of the tab in cash, and you guys split the rest of the bill? That makes it easy for everyone, and maybe a little more even all around."

Either approach accomplishes two goals: Don's letting Tom and Bob know what he is going to do, so at the restaurant no one will be surprised; and he's offering a reasonable solution rather than simply complaining about the problem. Result: Don ends up paying what's fair, and no one is embarrassed or confused. Problem solved.

There's another point to make here: Bob and Tom and their companions were a bit clueless, at best, about the awkward situation they were putting Don and Mary in. (At worst, they were taking advantage of Don and Mary, which is really bad news—and could be a sign that it's time to seek out some new friends.) The best solution would have been if someone else in the group had recognized the problem and suggested that the "even split" policy was no longer fair to Don and Mary. For example, Tom might have said to the waiter, "Do us a favor, please. Put fifty dollars on this [Don's] card, and split the rest between the other two cards. Thank you."

Tom should do this discreetly, without making a big deal about it. In return, Don should offer his and Mary's appreciation for Tom's understanding. Then everyone can sit back and enjoy a wonderful friendship.

Small Grossnesses

Fingers vs. Forks with Shared Plates of Food

"Let's share an appetizer sampler," you suggest. Your friends all agree enthusiastically, and soon a large plate of fried calamari, zucchini slices, and other delicious hors d'oeuvres arrives. You start to reach for a piece of calamari when, directly to your right, Jared suddenly turns away from the table and sneezes. He quickly wipes off his nose and hands, and then grabs a calamari with his fingers. You suddenly lose your appetite—for good reason. While it was nice of Jared to turn his head and avoid spraying the sampler, he still made two glaring mistakes. First, he failed to excuse himself from the table to wash his hands after sneezing. Second, he used his hands to take items from the sampler plate.

Then you realize, "I was about to take a calamari with my fingers, too—and nobody saw me picking my nose a few minutes ago."

You resolve, from now on, to start using a fork or serving utensil whenever you're eating from a shared plate. Score another victory for consideration-based etiquette!

Double Dipping

You're hosting a party, and you decide to make a special effort by serving a big platter of shrimp along with a bowl of cocktail sauce. Everyone gathers around for the feast. The procedure is simple: grab a shrimp, dip it in the sauce, and enjoy.

Then it happens: across from you Dainty Debbie takes a bite and then, to your horror, dips the uneaten portion *back into the sauce bowl* so she can have a little sauce with her next bite. Several other guests look at you and silently speculate: *"What's he going to do?"*

"Let me see if I can freshen up this plate," you say to no one in particular. You pick up the platter and go to the kitchen, where you spoon out the area where Debbie double dipped or, better yet, replace the sauce with some you still have left because you were smart enough to buy extra.

P.S. Don't even think about giving the sauce a quick stir. While this may seem to be the easy solution, it's worse than Debbie's double dipping.

If you really want to take the bull by the horns, ask Debbie if she can help you in taking the platter out. When you and Debbie get to the kitchen, ask her politely to please not double dip, and explain that by doing so she's making the shrimp unappetizing for some of the other

---

Etiquette Imperative

When addressing problematic behavior, your goal is never to embarrass, but to prevent the situation from recurring.

guests: "Debbie, I'm sure you didn't even know you were doing this, but . . ." The key is to do this quietly and privately.

Coughs, Sneezes, and Other Sudden Gusts

You can't stop a sneeze. But you can make an effort to avoid spreading your germs over the table. When I feel a sneeze coming on, I'll turn away and cover my mouth with my napkin. If the sneeze comes on fast, I'll at least bring my hands up to my face and look down into my lap as I sneeze. Then I'll excuse myself and head for the rest room to wash up. (If the sneeze turns into a sneezing fit, I'll go directly to the rest room to let it play itself out.)

The same goes for coughing: put hands to face, turn away if possible or at least look down, then excuse yourself and head to the rest room to wash up.

Burps and passing gas are largely a matter of self-control—so practice it. You can do it. I *know* you can. Simply excuse yourself and retire to the rest room. No explanations are necessary.

If a burp escapes by mistake, the proper response is to say, "I'm so sorry. It happened before I could stop it." Once in a long while, you can get away with this. Make it a habit, though, and you may find yourself eating alone.

If gas passes unexpectedly, this can be a bit more embarrassing. If the episode is silent and unnoticeable, count yourself lucky. If not, be prepared to apologize to your immediate neighbors: "Oh, my—I'm so embarrassed. Please excuse me." Even though you may be red-faced for a moment, you'll save your companions from the embarrassment of others thinking one of them is the culprit.

Don't Take What's Not Offered

Terry and her date went out for breakfast, and she ordered a fruit cup along with her eggs and bacon. Shortly after they had been served, he speared a piece of fruit from her fruit cup with his fork and ate it.

Terry was stunned. She hadn't offered him a taste of her food, and he certainly hadn't asked. Instead he just reached over and took a bite of her meal as if it were his own.

One word: don't.

When I discussed this situation with Terry, I suggested a couple of responses. She could either offer him the fruit cup, saying, "Tom, please have this fruit cup, I'll get another." Or she could offer to get him his own: "Tom, would you like some fruit? I'd be glad to ask the waiter to bring you a cup." Either way, she is benevolently sending him the message to stop taking food from her plate.

Offering a Taste

One of the pleasures of eating out is ordering different foods, and then sharing them. Sometimes, if I can't decide what to order, my wife will say, "Why don't you order the lamb; I'll get the curry? Then you can have a taste of mine."

When our food arrives, if my wife hasn't used her fork yet, she can use it now to prepare a bite for me and put it on the side of my plate. Alternatively, I can give her my fork and have her use it to prepare a small forkful for me. What I *don't* do is say, "Thanks, honey," and then help myself to the food on her plate.

15

Entertaining at Home

WHETHER YOU'RE HAPPILY MARRIED, or a single guy keeping house for yourself, there will invariably come a time when you want to invite guests over. The first prerequisite for entertaining at home is to have a *clean, orderly* residence where your guests will feel comfortable. This is true even if you're only planning to catch a ball game on television with your frat brothers. It's even more true if you are arranging an intimate, home-cooked meal for a special someone.

Here's the scenario: you ran into Monica two days ago at the coffee shop. You'd met her a few weeks earlier, when she came along with your friend Lisa to an ultimate Frisbee game at the local park. You talk ultimate Frisbee for a few minutes and laugh about the great time you all had. Then you pop the question: "Hey, Monica, I love to cook. Would you let me cook dinner for you sometime? Maybe we could take in that Scorcese movie afterward. I could even ask Jim and Lisa to join us and make it a foursome. Or not—it's up to you."

You're on a roll here. By offering to cook dinner for Monica, you're really showing off your best side. Then you ice the cake by suggesting that you invite another couple along, ensuring that she'll feel safe and comfortable coming over to your place for a date.

"Sounds great! I had a good time with Lisa—it'll be fun to see her again," Monica says with enthusiasm.

It's not until you're well on your way home that reality sets in. "What was I thinking?" you ask yourself. "My place is a pigsty, I don't *really* know how to cook, and I'd better make darn sure that Jim and Lisa can make it!"

Cleaning Up—The Right Way

First impressions are very hard to change—and this is Monica's first impression of how you live your life. Fail to clean up properly, and she'll have *that* introductory image burned in her mind forever.

Keeping your residence neat and clean isn't only about making good first impressions, of course. Maintaining a clean, livable home is a way of showing respect and consideration for anyone who stops in, from your next-door neighbor to your longtime girlfriend. If you've moved in with and/or married your longtime girlfriend, then doing your share of the house cleaning—without complaining or needing to be prompted—is one of the best ways you can show consideration for your wife or significant other. It also affords the two of you the freedom to welcome others to your home at any time.

Unfortunately, as I mentioned in chapter 2, when it comes to cleaning up, we men have a bad habit of thinking that it's okay to do a half-baked

Cleaning Up: The Bare Necessities

The first step in your transformation into Mr. Neat and Clean is to arm yourself with the basic cleaning supplies. Here are the bare necessities for keeping any man's home spotless:

General: Sponge, paper towels, vacuum, broom and dustpan, mop, bucket, rags (comprising old shirts, underwear, towels—clean, of course!)

Kitchen/Bathroom: Abrasive cleaner (Comet, Ajax), multipurpose cleaner (often with bleach or other antibacterial properties), dishwashing detergent

Windows/TV: Glass cleaner, paper towels or rag

Living Room/Den: Duster, wood polishers

job. But the fact is, cleaning your house the right way requires a complete and total commitment to finishing the job. When you clean your apartment, *really* clean it. Think of it as a business project—one that will automatically enhance the short-term value of your real estate, expand both your socializing and your networking options, and improve your day-to-day quality of life to boot.

Start by tackling the kitchen: scrub the counters; clean the stove surface; sweep the floor and mop thoroughly. Hit those areas you rarely think about: the refrigerator door, the splash spots around the stove and trashcan, even the inside of the microwave. I also strongly suggest cleaning out your refrigerator. (If your fridge is anything like ours, it's sure to contain any number of half-remembered items—in which case you should apply the time-tested principle: *when in doubt, throw it out!*)

Next, move on to your living room area: put away any papers, clothes, or sports equipment you have scattered around, then dust all surfaces, vacuum and/or sweep the floor, and straighten the furniture (don't forget to plump the pillows). Clean the less obvious places as well—like underneath all the seats and sofa cushions (snack food has a way of falling between the cracks) and behind the furniture (the other day I found the tail and head of a very dead mouse that one of our cats had thoughtfully left behind the couch!).

Now move on to the bedroom (even if you're not going to end up there at the end of your date, there's a good chance she'll catch a glimpse of it on the way to the bathroom): make the bed, put the dirty clothes in the hamper, and straighten up the bureau and shelf surfaces.

Last but far from least comes the bathroom. For this all-important room, refer back to our discussion in chapter 2. I'll simply remind you that in addition to cleaning your bathroom until it's immaculate, you should also remember to make sure you have a full roll of toilet paper on hand, along with a fresh set of hand towels and a fresh bar of soap in the soap dish. A scented candle with some matches and/or a spray deodorizer will also be a welcome touch.

Finally, if you have a cat, make sure the litter is fresh and doesn't smell; and if you have a dog, walk it before Monica and your other guests arrive.

My Wife's Simple Daily Cleaning Form

My wife has a passion for making lists—which I usually end up ignoring, I admit. But this one really works. She keeps it in a frame in the kitchen, where it serves as a daily guide.

DAILY CLEANING

Bedrooms

- Make bed
- Hang up clothes
- Put dirty clothes in hamper
- Put away books, projects
- Put away clean clothes

Bathroom

- Clean hair and scum from sink and shower
- Wipe sink and counter with sponge
- Put away toiletries
- Hang up towels
- Wipe off toilet

Living Areas

- Tidy up newspapers, magazines, and books
- Tidy up projects, videos, etc.
- Remove all dishes
- Straighten cushions, pillows

Kitchen

- Wash and put away dishes
- Empty/run dishwasher if needed
- Clean up spills immediately
- Wipe countertops
- Put away anything taken out
- Sort mail, put away books, coats, etc.

The K.I.S.S. School of Home Entertaining

If you're less than adept in the kitchen, then the value of the advice to "Keep It Simple, Stupid" will be self-evident: by doing a few things and doing them well, you'll spare yourself headaches and leave yourself free to concentrate on having a good time with your guests. But this advice also works if you're a gourmet cook, or if you're sharing the entertaining duties with your roommate, wife, or significant other. Trying to plan an overelaborate event is a surefire recipe for stress and conflict.

A simple agenda also makes it easier to divide up your entertaining

Etiquette Imperative

....

*You don't get credit for asking if you can help by doing something—
you get credit for <u>doing it</u>.*

....

chores. Decide ahead of time what each person's responsibilities will be for planning and hosting the event, then take the initiative in carrying out your own duties. Above all, never take the attitude that entertaining— including the food preparation—is primarily a woman's job. The preparations should *always* be a joint effort. When my wife and I entertain, we often trade off on the cooking, depending on the menu.

If your wife or significant other prefers to do the cooking, you can clean the patio, set up the bar, put in the dining room table extension, straighten the living room, and run the vacuum for a finishing touch. Another tip: don't simply walk in and ask, "What can I do?" Offer to do something specific—or even better, just start doing it. (This includes post-party cleanup!)

The K.I.S.S. Meal Plan

Before deciding on your menu, be sure to find out if any of your guests is vegetarian or has other dietary restrictions, including any food allergies. Next, plan a menu that allows you to do as much of the food preparation ahead of time as possible so you're free to focus on your guests.

K.I.S.S. Appetizers

For hors d'oeuvres, serve two or three types of cheese and some crackers; chips and salsa (medium or mild so you don't scorch a sensitive palate); or fresh veggies and some ranch dressing for a dip.

K.I.S.S. Main Course

Choose a menu that uses a few simple, delicious ingredients—preferably in a dish involving a minimum of pots and serving plates.

Don't be shy about asking friends and family for ideas—everyone has at least *one* favorite party recipe. My own follows: it fits all the K.I.S.S. criteria, is simple to make, uses only two pots, can be prepared ahead of

time, and makes you look like a culinary wizard. Best of all, you can prepare the chicken ahead of time, early in the afternoon. So instead of
spending time in the kitchen while your guests are at your home, you can
spend your time with them.

Chicken Tarragon with Tomatoes and Asparagus over Pasta for four
You will need:

- ➤ One per person: skinless, boneless chicken breasts or center-cut pork chops or veal cutlets

- ➤ 1 box of grape tomatoes or cherry tomatoes

- ➤ 6 to 8 stalks of asparagus per person

- ➤ Dried tarragon (in the spice section)

- ➤ Chicken broth, 16-ounce can

- ➤ 1 lemon

- ➤ 12-ounce box of egg noodles (in your grocer's pasta section)

- ➤ Flour for sifting

- ➤ 3 to 4 tablespoons of extra virgin olive oil

- ➤ Waxed paper

- ➤ Aluminum foil (if you don't have a skillet with a lid)

- ➤ Salt and pepper

- ➤ White wine (optional)

Usually chicken breasts come in one whole, two-breast piece. Cut the
breasts apart and trim off any visible fat. If you wish, you can further cut
the breasts lengthwise into two or three strips, to make smaller, more
manageable pieces.

Place a skillet with a lid (if you don't have a lid for your skillet or frying
pan, make one out of a piece of aluminum foil) on a burner set to
medium-high heat. Add 3 to 4 tablespoons of olive oil, enough to easily
cover the bottom of the skillet.

While the oil heats, lay the chicken pieces on a sheet of the waxed
paper. Dust the tops with flour and ground pepper. When the skillet is
hot, place the pieces in the skillet floured side down. Let the chicken

brown for 3 to 4 minutes. While the first side is browning, sprinkle a thin coating of flour and pepper onto the faceup sides. Turn and brown the second side for 3 to 5 minutes. (If you want, you can shake a little salt onto the browned side of the chicken.)

After the second side has browned, pour the broth into the skillet. I try to use enough so the chicken is about half in and half out of the broth. (If you like, you can use white wine in place of about one quarter of the chicken broth.)

Next, sprinkle a tablespoon of tarragon over the chicken pieces, then squeeze the juice from a slice of lemon over the chicken. Turn down the heat to low or simmer and cover. Let the contents simmer 20 to 30 minutes. If you are preparing this dish early in the afternoon, turn off the heat after 30 minutes and let it sit with the cover on until cool enough to refrigerate (you can reheat it in about 20 minutes on simmer before serving).

While the chicken is cooking, wash the tomatoes and asparagus. Cut the tomatoes in half and put them in a bowl, and cut the tough bottoms off the stalks of asparagus.

Twenty minutes before you want to eat, fill a large pot with water and bring it to a boil.

When the chicken has 10 minutes left to cook, or 10 minutes before you want to eat it, add the tomatoes and the asparagus to the skillet and continue to simmer for 10 more minutes. Add the noodles to the water and cook them for the length of time indicated on the package.

When the noodles are cooked, turn off all the burners and drain the noodles in a colander. Uncover the chicken. Serve the noodles and portions of chicken, tomatoes, and asparagus directly on each plate, then spoon the remaining sauce over the chicken and noodles.

K.I.S.S. Dessert

For dessert: cookies and ice cream; a pie from a local bakery; fresh fruit. There are great pastry and bakery shops out there in most communities; you're sure to find something delicious while sparing yourself a ton of work.

Last-Minute Details

Use the hour before your guests are due to arrive to go over all the final touches: make sure that the table is set properly, the white wine or beer is chilled, the ice bucket is filled, the lemons and limes are sliced, the music is ready to play, and the serving area is organized so that when the food is ready it gets to the table *before* it gets cold. Lighted candles are always a fine scene-setter. Now, take a moment to put your feet up, have a look around, and take in the warm, inviting scene. At the very least, your guests will be completely bowled over by the care and time you've put in on their behalf. Most likely, you'll all have a memorable time. And Monica? Let's just say that, at the very least, your relationship will be getting off on the right foot!

The Perfect Host

Fifteen years before Emily Post wrote her first etiquette book, when she was still famous mainly as the bestselling author of romantic fiction, she defined the perfect host in one of her novels. The book, *The Title Market,* is set in Rome in the early 1900s. The scene describes an Italian princess hosting a party at her home:

> Throughout the evening there was the simplest sort of buffet supper: teas, bouillon—a claret cup, perhaps, and chocolate, little cakes, and sandwiches; never more. But the princess was one of those hostesses whose personality thoroughly pervades a house; a type which is becoming rare with every change in our modern civilization, and without which people might as well congregate in a hotel parlor. Each guest at the Palazzo Sansevero carried away the impression that not only had he been welcome himself, but that his presence had added materially to the enjoyment of others.

A clean home, great food, pleasant music—these elements all contribute to a great evening. But the one element that really makes or breaks a gathering at your home is you—the host. It's your job to make sure that everyone feels welcome and to be attentive to each and every guest:

➤ Greet guests when they arrive

➤ Circulate among your guests, introduce strangers, and stay long enough to get a conversation started

➤ Keep an eye on your guests and offer to refill drinks as needed

➤ Make sure the appetizer plates are replenished as needed

If you accomplish these things, the occasion is guaranteed to be a success for everyone involved.

"May I Bring Something?"

Often a guest will ask if he or she can bring something to a party or event, or help out in some other way. In fact, a thoughtful guest will *always* make this offer. However, this does *not* make it okay for you to invite someone, and then—*after* they've accepted the invitation—ask them to bring something. The only time you can ask a guest to contribute is if you also make it clear, as you're extending the invitation, that everyone is providing a dish or beverage of some sort. That way, the person being invited has the opportunity to turn the invitation down if they prefer.

By the same token, just because a guest offers to bring something to your party *doesn't* mean you have to take them up on the offer. You have every right to simply say, "Thanks, but everything's taken care of. Just bring yourselves, and have a good time!"

A considerate guest will take you at your word. If the other person simply won't take no for an answer, you can always suggest that they bring a bottle of wine—though again, you're not under any obligation to serve their wine that night.

If you're visiting someone else's home, the same principle works in reverse: unless the event you've been invited to is a formal occasion such as a wedding or a bar mitzvah, you should *always* ask if you can help out, either by bringing something or by pitching in on the preparations or cleanup.

Your hosts may welcome your contribution—in fact, the assistance of friends can often make all the difference. If, on the other hand, they tell you not to bring anything, believe them! Above all, *don't* show up with any unasked-for food. It's your hosts' meal to plan, not yours.

If your hosts don't take you up on your offer and you still feel you *must* bring something, I suggest bringing some flowers—which are always welcome, and which enhance the evening without affecting the menu.

Etiquette Imperative

Unless it's a potluck affair, a thoughtful host <u>never</u> asks his guests to bring anything. And unless it's a formal occasion, a thoughtful guest <u>always</u> volunteers to bring something.

An alternative to flowers is a bottle of wine. If you bring wine, explain that the wine is for your hosts' enjoyment anytime they like, and that you aren't expecting them to serve it that evening.

Potluck or Group Parties

Starting an informal, potluck tradition is a wonderful way for a group of friends or relatives to sustain their bonds over time, since the responsibility is a shared one, and the party's success is something everyone can bask in. For example: over the past few years we've helped organize several monster clambakes on Martha's Vineyard. We dig a pit in the sand, line it with old iron cannonballs saved just for this purpose, and build a huge fire in the pit to heat the cannonballs. When they're red hot, we remove the fire and fill the pit with rockweed, lobsters, corn on the cob, onions, sweet potatoes, crabs, and anything else we can think of. Then we cover it all with a big canvas tarp and let the food cook for three hours.

We've had as many as seventy-five people show up for the event. They all contribute with money, food, and brawn. By the end of the evening, black bags filled with garbage are loaded into each S.U.V. When we leave, you wouldn't know any event had ever taken place.

There's no way one or two people could pull this sort of party off. For our clambake to be a success (and it must be, because people are always asking when we're going to organize the next one), it takes the willingness of everyone to pitch in.

16

······································

Dinnertime

EMILY POST ONCE WROTE: *"All the rules of table manners are made to avoid ugliness. To let anyone see what you have in your mouth is repulsive; to make a noise is to suggest an animal; to make a mess is disgusting."*

Viewed objectively, the act of eating is inherently a somewhat, well, gross activity. Think about it: the key to good eating etiquette is to bite, chew, and swallow without offending the people around you. Of course, none of us are bothered by our *own* eating habits—but when the guy across the table takes an enormous bite of hamburger, chews with his mouth open, or talks with his mouth full, the result is disgusting, plain and simple.

If you're not sure how you look when you eat, try placing a mirror on the table one night and watching yourself. Believe me, the effort is worth it. Nothing unimpresses quite so quickly as bad table manners and sloppy eating behavior.

Nowhere are poor table manners more evident than at a formal dinner. But good table manners aren't something you can simply switch on when the occasion warrants. Instead, they need to be practiced every day—even if you're dining on pizza alone in your kitchen—so that they become an ingrained habit.

The Three Most-Asked Questions About Table Manners

1. **How should you hold and use your knife and fork?** The question here really is about the correct technique of using utensils: the American style (in which the diner cuts meat with the fork in his left hand and then switches the fork to his right hand to bring the cut meat to his mouth) or the continental style (in which the fork always stays in the left hand)?

   Some Americans complain about people who eat their food continental-style. "It's pretentious," they complain. Nonsense. The only thing "pretentious" is somebody who thinks that there's only one acceptable dining style. Personally, I've always eaten continental style: I think it's easier than switching the fork back and forth. Nobody taught me to do it—the technique just seemed natural to me.

   So the real answer to this question is: it doesn't matter! Either style is acceptable. Do what's most comfortable for you.

   In her book on etiquette, Emily Post called the American style "zig-zag" eating and then observed wryly: "Why an able-bodied person should like to pretend that the left hand is paralyzed and cannot be lifted more than three or four inches above the table is beyond understanding."

2. **Can you put your elbows on the table?** For a long time, the ironclad rule was: *no elbows on the table.* I learned my etiquette (such as it is) from my father, who was Emily Post's grandson, and my mother, who spent thirty years writing and revising the Emily Post etiquette books. Apparently they never heard of this particular rule—because in our home, I saw elbows on the table all the time.

   The real issue here is how to sit at a table and not look like a slob. If you sit at the table hunched over your plate, leaning on your elbows, and shoveling food into your mouth, then the "no elbows on the table" rule is the least of your problems. If for no other reason, I don't put my elbows on the tabletop simply because it isn't practical to eat with them on the table.

Between courses, however, when I'm conversing with a companion, I may lean toward the table with my elbows propped on the edge of the table and my hands clasped together. Leaning forward in this fashion is one way of showing your attention to the person you are with. I've also watched two lovebirds, during a romantic moment between courses, each stretch an arm across the table, the elbow resting on the table, to hold hands for a minute. I am certainly *not* going to rap them on the elbows and tell them they're breaking a "rule."

Bottom line: use common sense. An elbow resting gently on the table between courses shouldn't offend anyone. The one exception to this is when you're a guest. Whether it's a meal at your in-laws' home or a fancy, highbrow dinner party, before you start using the table as an elbow rest, take a look at the other guests and follow their example.

3. **What's the correct direction to pass food at a table?** Pass to the right.

The reason for this rule probably lies in the fact that we live in a right-hand-dominated society. When you pass food to the right, you automatically place the dish in the receiving person's left hand. They can then easily serve themselves with their free right hand. (If the dish is especially heavy or large—like a salad bowl, for example—you may want to offer to hold it for the person on your right while she serves herself.)

Passing in one direction also prevents a log jam from happening as platters or baskets come at you from both directions.

When to Pass to the Left

When plates of food are passed around the table, they are passed to the right. But what happens when you are at a table of eight or ten people and the person two seats to your left asks for the bread?

Pass the bread to the left. Making it go the long way around the table would be ridiculous.

Your Task as a Guest or a Host

To return to Emily's observation at the start of this chapter, if you simply think about making choices at the table that allow you to avoid being ugly, repulsive, or disgusting, you'll most likely display very good table manners. But the real task of the host and the guest is to be a good conversationalist, a good neighbor, and a good participant. Be sure to talk with the people on either side of you at the table. *Participate* in conversations by asking questions and making pleasant comments, but don't try to *dominate* the conversation or impose your views on others, and steer away from controversial topics. Remember, the goal is for everyone to have a lively and fun time.

A Quick Journey Through a Formal Dinner

Arriving at the Table

If you're a guest, look for your place card. If there isn't one, wait for the host to indicate where you should sit.

When you get to your place, remain standing and offer to hold the chairs for the women sitting to either side of you. Once the hostess has taken her seat, or as the host sits down, you may sit.

Immediately place your napkin on your lap. Don't tuck it into your shirt or belt or shake it out to unfold it. Just lay it on your lap.

If you don't know the people seated on either side of you, introduce yourself (for tips on introductions, see chapter 7). Depending on how big the table is, you should also nod and say hello to any other people in your vicinity.

The Place Setting

Intimidated by all those glasses and all that silverware? Not to worry: they've actually been placed with great care, to make it easy for you to know when to use which item.

You'll find knives and spoons on the right side of your plate, and forks on the left. (The only exception is an oyster fork, which will be on the right. This fork is used for oysters, raw clams, or shrimp cocktail.) The correct order of use is *from the outside in*. This way, the outlying utensils are gradually stripped away as the meal progresses, leaving the utensil for the next course on the outside of the place setting.

Some restaurants think they are being fancy by setting the dessert spoon and fork at the top of the place setting (the fork closer to you and with its handle pointing to the left, the spoon further away with the handle pointing to the right.) You can't control what restaurants do, but when you're setting a table at home, especially for a formal meal, the dessert spoon and fork should *not* be part of the table setting. It's more appropriate to have them accompany the dessert.

Your glassware is set to the right side of your table setting, just above the knives and spoons. The types of glasses used will vary depending on what beverages are going to be served. The glasses are arrayed in descending size, from left to right. The water glass—the largest—is on the far left. To its right comes the red wine glass, then the white wine glass, followed (in theory) by a champagne glass and a sherry glass. Of course, that's a lot of glasses! It's more common to have a water glass, a red wine glass, and a white wine glass arranged from left to right.

The butter plate and butter knife (if there is one) are set above the forks on the left side of your place setting. The butter knife is typically placed on the edge of the butter plate.

If you don't order a particular course at a restaurant, the waiter will remove the utensils that would ordinarily be used for that course, so you will have the proper utensils for the next course on the outside of the place setting.

During the Meal

Don't toss your tie over your shoulder to keep from dribbling on it.

Do hold the red wine glass by the bowl. It's easier to balance it that way, and the warmth from your hand won't affect the wine. However, always hold your white wine glass by the stem, to prevent your body heat from taking the chill off the wine.

Nose blowing: a quick wipe in an emergency is okay, but true nose blowing should happen in the rest room.

Yes, you *may* tip your soup bowl to spoon up that last bit of soup. At a formal dinner, tip the bowl away from you, and fill your spoon with a motion that moves your spoon away from your body—not to be pretentious, but to avoid splattering your clothes.

At the completion of the soup course, if the soup bowl is a shallow

Cheap Restaurants

You would think managers of restaurants would know better. In the name of lower costs, the wait staff are often told to take a knife (and sometimes even a fork) that you have already used and left on your salad plate, and place the same utensil back on the table for use with the next course.

I'm sorry, but this is totally revolting, not to mention unsanitary. If everyone agreed to rebel whenever this occurs, maybe we could stop restaurants from instituting such a disgusting procedure. When this happens to me, I always ask the waiter to bring me clean utensils. Sometimes they'll actually try to argue with me. And all to save having to wash an extra set of utensils. Talk about lousy service!

one, leave the spoon in the bowl with the handle pointing to the right. If it's a deep bowl and there is a plate under it, place the spoon on the edge of the plate, again with the handle pointing to the right.

Never put a dirty utensil directly onto the table.

There are two opposing rules about when to start eating. Emily believed in enjoying a meal while it was still warm. Following this philosophy, when you're with a group of friends in a relaxed situation, it's acceptable to begin eating once at least three people have been served. In a more formal situation or at a business meal, however, you should wait until everyone has been served, or until the host or hostess says something like, "Please start right away. Don't let your food get cold waiting for ours to be served."

If you are the host, once three plates have been served, let the people who have been served know that it's all right for them to start. As Emily noted, it would be a shame to let that delicious food start cooling, just because every guest hasn't been served yet.

When you need salt and/or pepper, always ask for both. Likewise, if someone asks you for "the salt," pass both.

Don't salt or pepper your food until *after* you've tasted it. Once I mistakenly salted split pea soup before tasting it. Turns out it was salty to begin with. After I finished salting it, it was inedible.

If you want to take a break from eating, simply place your knife and fork on the plate with the tip of the knife and the tines of the fork positioned at the top of your plate. Tines up or tines down? Knife blade facing one way or the other? It doesn't really matter—just do it neatly, and you'll be fine.

I can't stand to leave a really good sauce sitting on a plate. But use bread to mop up that fantastic sauce, not your fingers. Break off a small piece of bread, then use your fork to push the bread around in the left-over sauce and then bring the morsel to your mouth.

When you're cutting your meat, slice off one bite-size piece, eat it, then cut the next piece. Unless you're preparing a plate for a young child, *don't* cut a whole steak into bite-sized pieces and then start eating.

If you need to leave the table during the meal, gently fold your napkin so that any soiled parts are covered, then lay it on the table to the left of your place setting. Do the same thing when you leave the table at the conclusion of the meal.

At the end of each course, picture your plate as a clock. Then place your knife and fork on your plate side by side in the four o'clock position. Don't get anal about whether your dinner partner "made a mistake" because he or she placed the fork above the knife, or left the blade of the knife facing away from the fork. If you are that focused on other people's faux pas, then you're missing the real point of good table manners and formal dinners, which is to enjoy the company you are with.

Dessert arrives. As the host, you've made the choice to serve dessert at the table. You cut the first piece of black forest cake and place it on the nearest plate. As you do, some frosting gets on your finger. "Man, it looks good," you think to yourself. "What about just a quick lick?" *Don't do it.* Either wipe your fingers on a napkin, or keep serving as if nothing happened.

If wine or coffee is being served and you don't care for any, don't turn your glass or cup over. Simply tell the server, "No, thank you." If you are served anyway, simply leave the glass or cup alone and go back to your conversation, which is much more important, anyway.

At Dinner's End

As a guest, don't take it upon yourself to call a close to the evening. As you've done throughout the evening, take your cues as to the proper time to leave from the other guests and from your host.

When the time comes for you to bid farewell, thank your host for a special evening with all the warmth and sincerity you can muster. Also, make sure to say good night to the people who were sitting on either side of you and to the other diners who were near you at the table.

Finally, when you get home that evening, take a few minutes to write a brief thank-you note of three to five sentences to your host. Address and stamp the envelope, and put the note in a place where you'll see it and remember to mail it the next morning. Your host will appreciate your thoughtfulness, and you will have cemented your reputation as an engaged, gracious dinner guest—ensuring that you'll get invited back again.

17

The Houseguest from Hell

YOU KNOW WHO I'M talking about: that out-of-town visitor who leaves a trail of belongings around the house, ties up the phone, leaves his or her children with you as though you were running a baby-sitting agency, puts down roots in your sofa, or—worst of all—doesn't know when to leave.

Of course, spotting the things that someone *else* is doing wrong is easy. It's a lot more difficult to admit the ways in which *you* may be ruffling your hosts' feathers when *you* are the overnight visitor. As you read about the following houseguest-from-hell behaviors, take a look in the mirror and ask if you see yourself in any of these situations.

The Etiquette of Visiting: Be Clean and Helpful— and Share the Remote!

According to our Post Survey, the single biggest factor that turns an ordinary houseguest into the Houseguest from Hell is failing to clean up. Topping the list of complaints were: scattering dirty clothes on the floor; leaving shaving stubble and hair in the sink; failing to hang towels on the towel rack; leaving the bed unmade; using dishes and then not washing them; and failing to wipe shoes before entering the home.

Other issues that sparked our respondents' ire included:

BEING DISRESPECTFUL. The complaints in this category centered on guests who simply go over the line, by . . .

➤ Expecting the host(ess) to wait on them hand and foot

➤ Bragging and acting self-centered

➤ Ignoring the host or hostess

➤ Inviting friends over without asking first

➤ Showing up with an unannounced companion, child, or pet

➤ Putting feet on the furniture

➤ Being downright rude

➤ Staying too long

➤ Walking around the house unclothed or clad only in underwear

THE TOILET. In our survey, one out of seven houseguest complaints mentioned the toilet. Most of these involved the infamous problem of leaving the toilet seat up—but we also received numerous comments about poor aim.

BEING UNHELPFUL. Complaints included failing to help to clear plates from the table, not pitching in with the dishes, and never offering to help with household chores.

HOGGING THE TELEVISION. In particular, our respondents complained about houseguests who turn into couch potatoes upon their arrival, insist on watching nothing but sports, or who sit clutching the remote, not allowing anyone else near it.

Houseguest "Danger Zones"

When you're staying overnight with friends or family, there are three areas where even the tidiest, most helpful houseguest can run into trouble: the telephone, the refrigerator, and the car.

The Phone

I have heard numerous horror stories of houseguests running up huge long-distance phone tabs, which their hosts only discover a few weeks later when the bill arrives. Using the phone to make a long-distance call without asking permission first is no different from stealing money from your host's wallet.

If you have your own cell phone, use it. Otherwise, bring a prepaid phone card with you (many are now available that cost just a few cents per minute), or use the calling card supplied by your own long-distance carrier. If you have no cell phone or calling card, first ask permission to use the phone—and then be sure to give your host enough cash to cover the cost of your call.

The Refrigerator

As they like to say in South America, *mi casa es su casa*. My house is your house. A welcome sentiment, but one that houseguests should be careful not to take too literally, especially where the refrigerator is concerned. Example: when Jeb arrives, Jan shows him around the place. "And here's the fridge," she says as they enter the kitchen. "Feel free to help yourself, but please, leave the pies. They're for dinner tomorrow night." While she's speaking, she carefully points out the item(s) that are off-limits.

Instead, let's suppose that Jan never mentioned the pies. Late that night, Hungry Jeb pads into the kitchen looking for a little snack, opens the fridge, and sees a beautiful pie sitting there just begging to be eaten. Smart Jeb thinks to himself, "Hmm, that pie looks good—too good to just be there for the taking." So Smart Jeb passes on the pie, grabs some cookies and milk instead, and goes back to bed, where he dreams of the pie to come the next day.

The Car

Mi casa es su casa is especially problematic where automobiles are concerned. Another example: when Jeb first arrives, Dan tells him, "Don't be shy, Jeb. Think of this as your house, too." When Jeb realizes a few hours later that he's forgotten his shaving cream, he thinks, "I won't bother Dan and Jan. *Mi casa es su casa.* I'll just borrow their new BMW, and get it myself."

Lots of things can go wrong with this plan: Dan could finish his business in the bathroom, head outside to get the paper, and notice that the BMW is gone. Thinking it's been stolen, he calls the police. Result: Jeb gets pulled over. Or worse, while Jeb is in the store, another driver cuts it too close while pulling out of the space next to the BMW and scrapes the car badly. Note to Jeb: that's one expensive can of shaving cream.

When it comes to your hosts' car, borrow only when absolutely necessary—and *always* ask permission first.

The Five Keys to a Successful Visit

These five guidelines will spell the difference between a successful visit and a friendship turned sour.

1. **ESTABLISH A DEFINITE TIME LIMIT FOR THE VISIT WHEN THE INVITATION IS MADE.** Friendly Fred thought he was doing the right thing by inviting his old college friend Bill to stay with him for a couple of weeks. Bill had recently lost his job and was thinking about moving to Fred's city.

   "It'll be like old college times in the dorm," Fred told Bill.

   Now, a month later, Furious Fred is ready to hogtie Bill and throw him out on his ear. Bill has moved in lock, stock, and barrel, and Fred can't budge him. He even tried announcing that he was going away for a week, and Bill countered by saying that he would be happy to water the plants and feed the fish while Fred was away. It was the least he could do, he acknowledged.

   Fred made the classic mistake: he extended an invitation with no preset time limit. If you invite someone to stay at your home, *set a definite time frame at the time you make the invitation.* Conversely, if you're planning a visit and your host tells you to stay "as long as you like," gently explain that you really have to be back home at a certain, fixed date.

Here's how Fred *should* have worded his offer to Bill:

"Why don't you come stay with me for a few days? You could stay until next Wednesday morning. We'll have the weekend to catch up, and you can check out the job opportunities on Monday and Tuesday. By Wednesday, you should have a good idea whether there is anything here worth pursuing."

Then, midway through Bill's visit, Fred says, "Hey, Bill, I'm trying to set up my schedule for Wednesday. How about if I give you a ride to the train station on my way to work?"

If Bill replies that he's thinking of staying longer, then Fred needs to put his heels into the ground and reply, "That's great, and I've enjoyed our visit, but Wednesday is as long as I can have you stay here, Bill. If you're planning on staying longer, you'll need to find another place. I'm sure you understand."

Of course, Bill being who he is, Fred then needs to stick to his plan like white on rice.

2. BRING A HOUSE PRESENT. People frequently ask me, "Do I have to bring a present every time I'm visiting someone overnight?"

"Yes," I answer. The gift needn't be grandiose—just something that says, "Thank you for inviting me into your home." For an overnight or weekend stay, plants or flowers are always a

Gift Suggestions for a Longer Stay

When the visit will be longer than an overnight or weekend, you may want to consider a larger gift such as:

➢ A breakfast basket from a local gourmet shop that could include pancake mix, bacon or Canadian ham, and real Vermont maple syrup.

➢ Fixings for an ice cream sundae party (especially good if kids are involved). For a visit with friends in the Adirondacks, we filled a basket with a variety of syrups and toppings, a couple of cans of Redi-Whip, and a small ice cream maker.

➢ A set of monogrammed beach towels. Great for a summer vacation visit to the beach or if the hosts have a pool.

good idea (silk flowers are okay, as well). Another gift that I really like is a coffee-table book—one that's fun to read with lots of pictures, either on a subject you know your hosts are interested in (a photo-history of cricket, for example), or on a subject that you're interested in and that you think your hosts would enjoy learning more about (such as a book on the architecture of Italy). Finally, a box of chocolates is also nice—provided your hosts aren't on a diet. I *don't* recommend bringing a bottle of wine. Wine is an appropriate gift for a dinner party, but not as a houseguest present.

3. GO WITH THE FLOW. Today's the day: Jeb has finally made his long-promised visit to Dan and Jan at their vacation house at

---

Meet the Parents

Oh, those awkward first moments when you're meeting the parents of your significant other for the first time. Should you introduce yourself to them? How do you greet them—with a hug or a handshake? And what should you call them?

Here's the scenario: Dan and Jan are planning to visit Jan's parents for the weekend—the first time Dan has ever met them, much less stayed with them.

The front door swings open.

"Jan, honey, you made it! We're so glad to see you . . ." and on it goes: hugs and kisses for Jan. Then it's Dan's turn.

Jan starts out: "Mom, Dad [remembering that you always address the more important person first when making an introduction—and in this case, even though Dan is the light of her life, she shows ultimate respect for her parents by talking to them first], I'd like to introduce Dan Petrified to you."

Next, Jan turns to Dan and says, "Dan, these are my parents, Tim and Heather."

And now Dan faces the *big* question: Is it "Tim" and "Heather," or is it Mr. and Mrs. Nervous?

It's Mr. and Mrs. Nervous, no question about it. Dan leads off with the formal, ultra-respectful form of address. He says, "I'm pleased to meet you, Mr. and Mrs. Nervous." Ninety-nine times out of one hundred, Mr. or Mrs. Nervous will respond, "Oh, Dan, we're so glad to finally meet you. Jan's told us so much about you. And please—it's Tim and Heather."

the New Jersey shore. It's the first morning after his arrival, and the sun is already high in the sky when he ambles down the stairs, his head filled with thoughts of the beach, swimming, bikinis, and lots of nothing to do.

"Hey, Jeb, you old sack hound," Dan says, putting down the morning paper. "Today's the day: the cricket match finals are only thirty minutes from here, and we've got front-row seats. You've got just enough time for a shower and a cup of coffee, then we've got to hit the road."

Cricket matches? What happened to the beach and the swimming and the bikinis?

Answer: *When in Rome, do as the Romans do.* When you're a houseguest, you go with the program—cricket matches and all. Suddenly, Jeb sees his plans for fun in the sun vanish. Within a few minutes, though, he is showered, caffeinated, and ready to go:

"So, Jan, what's cricket all about? If you guys are into this sport, there *must* be something to it. Tell me more . . ."

4. **MAKE AN EFFORT TO CONTRIBUTE.** Simple acts of contribution make all the difference in the world—like helping with the dishes, straightening the furniture in the living room before you go to bed, wiping down the bathroom after showering and / or shaving, or offering to chop vegetables before dinner. In particular, make an effort to help with the tasks that are a part of your visit.

5. **THANK YOUR HOSTS TWICE.** The first time you thank them is when you're ready to leave: "I had a great time," Jeb tells Dan and Jan, as the taxi that will take him to the airport idles nearby. "I can't thank you enough for your hospitality—not to mention the great food. You'll have to let me return the favor by hosting you at my house in Milwaukee. There's no beach, of course— but there are some restaurants I know you'll love!"

The second thank-you should be sent by mail, as soon as you arrive back home.

A Sample Thank-You Note

Dear Dan and Jan,

I can't thank you enough for the great time I had visiting you at the shore. The cricket match was so unexpected, and made for such a fun day. I had no idea the sport could be so riveting!

Dan, you were right—the beach and the swimming and the scenery make your place a terrific getaway! I'm more relaxed now than I have been in months.

Jan, the party you threw on Saturday night was fantastic. And the *pie*! Dan has probably told you that I'm a sucker for strawberry pie, and yours was the best I've ever tasted!

Thank you both for showing me such a great time. I hope you can make it out to Milwaukee for a visit sometime this fall.

Best to you both,

Jeb

18

To Flirt or Not to Flirt?

L ET'S CUT STRAIGHT TO the heart of the matter: forget the word *flirting*. The underlying issue is *your intent*. Specifically, I'm talking about whether or not you've struck up a conversation with another person *with the intent of starting a personal, one-on-one, evolving, and <u>potentially intimate</u> relationship with that person.*

If the answer to this is yes, then you're flirting—and you are immediately subject to flirting etiquette, as follows:

> ➤ As long as *neither person is married or in a serious relationship*, then this kind of behavior is perfectly acceptable.

> ➤ If this sort of behavior is undertaken by two people, one or both of whom *is* married or in a serious relationship, then it's unacceptable.

In the course of my normal social life, I banter, joke, converse, enjoy innuendo, and indulge in fun, engaging, relaxed, and sometimes even racy conversations. By my definition, however, I am *not* flirting with the women (or the men, for that matter) with whom I am talking. Why? Because I have no intention of taking things any further than that particular conversation. In fact—and this is very important—nothing I do or

SURVEY SAYS
Attached? Don't Flirt!

On this topic, the Post Survey was overwhelmingly clear: 83 percent of our respondents agreed that married men are *not* given the green light to flirt. When we asked whether it was acceptable for a man who is in a serious relationship to flirt with another woman, almost the same proportion—79 percent—said no again.

Men who are simply dating, on the other hand, were given much more latitude: 66 percent of our respondents agreed that it was okay for them to flirt with whomever they wished. Unattached men, meanwhile, received the go-ahead to flirt by a whopping 88 percent of those who completed the survey.

say in these conversations involves anything I'd be embarrassed to tell my wife about later or have her hear at the time.

When Flirting Is Okay:
The Secrets of Successful Flirtation

Flirting is behavior that says, "I'm interested in you." That's why it is acceptable only for people who are playing the field or casually dating. Remember, the goal is to start a relationship. Much of the advice dispensed by flirting experts is really etiquette advice in disguise and involves the same essential elements: consideration, respect, and honesty.

With that in mind, here are some tips on what it takes to be a "successful" flirt:

Before You Start

Do a self-check: Are you clean? Is your breath fresh? Are your clothes appropriate for the occasion? Are you conveying a positive attitude? The image you're projecting determines what the other person will think of you. That's not to say you should put on an act. A critical component of etiquette is being sincere in whatever you do. People sense insincerity immediately, and it's a turn-off. So be your best self: positive, excited about the world around you, standing tall, engaging others confidently—and smiling.

First: Smile and Make Eye Contact

Flirting starts when you signal your interest in another person, or vice versa. This can be something as simple as smiling at someone, or having your smile returned. To get that returned smile, of course, you have to risk smiling yourself. Now you've begun.

Second: The Opening Line

Now you face the biggest hurdle in flirting: what to say first. Contrary to what all those books on dating would have you believe, there are no perfect one-liners—so forget about trying to memorize twenty sure-fire opening lines. They'll sound insincere, since you're *being* insincere, and you'll go down swinging.

When I'm giving public relations advice to my clients, I like to tell them: "When all else fails, try honesty. You'll be amazed at how well it works." And in the singles-bar world of "opening lines," a little self-effacing honesty often works wonders when it comes to breaking down barriers. A couple of examples:

THE DIRECT APPROACH. "I can't believe I'm doing this—but my name's Peter, and I was really hoping to have a chance to meet you."

THE INDIRECT APPROACH. You: "Hi."
Other person: "Hi."
You: "Nice band, huh?"
Other person: "Yeah."
You: "Hey, my name's Peter. How do you know Tom [the host]?"
If the other person responds, then the door is open. All you need to do is walk on through.

Third: Make Conversation

Once you've initiated a conversation and she's responded, what do you say next that is going to be interesting? Anyone can talk about the weather, but to make an impression, you need to do two things:

PREPARE IN ADVANCE. This means being up to speed on politics, current events, people in the news, sports, entertainment, music, popular books, movies—the works. Make it a habit to find information in a vari-

Flirting Pitfalls

Steer clear of opening gambits and conversational blunders that are immediate turnoffs. Religion and politics top the list. Avoid making direct comments about the other person ("Hey, beautiful"), don't be disrespectful toward her date, and *never* assume anything ("What do you say you and I have a party of our own? Your place or mine?").

ety of sources: the daily paper, magazines, radio and television news shows, and the entertainment news shows. Your preparation phase is also a great excuse to go to the movies and to expand your musical horizons: pop, rock, jazz, classical, you name it, and there's a woman out there interested in it.

Next, before you head out to the party or event, consciously think of several comments you're prepared to make on topics that interest you:

"Did you see the announcement yesterday? Phish is back! Is that great, or what?"

"I saw the most amazing deal last night. You can fly to London for $199, round-trip! I'm thinking of going for a long weekend. Have you ever been to London?"

PRACTICE TALKING TO STRANGERS. When you do get to this hurdle, you don't freeze. Chat with cab drivers, delivery people, the person at the checkout counter at your local grocery store . . . the list is endless.

Fourth: Be Aware

As you proceed, hurdle by hurdle, be alert to signals from the other person. Your efforts won't always be successful, and you need to be prepared to accept these signals gracefully and move on. For example, you might try the Phish line as an opening gambit, only to discover that she cares passionately about the classical flute and obviously isn't interested in talking music with a Phishhead. In that case you smile and reply, "Have fun! It was nice meeting you."

If you want to play in the game, you have to be willing to risk losing some of the time. This works both ways, of course. If it's you who is doing the rejecting, do it with class: "It's been really nice talking to you, but I see Tom over there, and I haven't talked to him in ages. Will you excuse me, please? Thanks!"

Fifth: Engage and Listen

Once the conversation has gotten rolling, don't just stand there spouting your opinions. Ask your conversation partner for her opinion, and then listen to her answer. Listening is a great way to show someone you are interested in them. Throughout the Post Survey, our female respondents extolled the virtues of men who *listen* to them.

Other conversation tips:

> Look the other person in the eye.

> Use body language to lean forward (but not too close, or you'll make her uncomfortable—eighteen inches is a good distance to maintain).

> Smile and nod your head as she's talking.

> For goodness sake, *don't interrupt.*

> React attentively to what she says: "I didn't know that," or "What an interesting idea," or "I really like classical flute, too—but when the Moody Blues brought electric flute into rock, that was outrageous!"

Sixth: Circulate

Whenever you're attending a party or event, you should always make an effort to circulate. Don't cling all night to the first person you make contact with. Instead, talk to as many different people as you can. The more you force yourself to mix and mingle, the easier it becomes. At the

Choose Your Location Carefully

Listening is a great skill, but first you've got to be able to hear a person. Bars with music so loud you can't hear yourself think may not be the most conducive places to try to start a conversation, at least not while the music is playing. Think before you act, and make sure that if you start a conversation, you're going to be able to continue it.

same time, your hosts and the other guests will appreciate your ability to socialize with lots of different people. That's what makes parties fun.

When You and Your Partner Disagree

What happens when *you* assume that your racy conversation with that female aerobics instructor at the health club wine-and-cheese social was perfectly okay, but your wife or significant other, watching from across the room, perceives your banter as a blatant come-on? Answer: you've got a problem that needs resolving—and quickly.

Simply put, if one person in a serious relationship feels that the other partner's behavior is straying over the line, that opinion must be respected—and the "flirtatious" partner needs to start revising his or her behavior in a way that you *both* find acceptable. It's an issue worth talking about openly with your partner: remember, strong, trusting relationships are built on honest communication, which entails clearly saying what you both mean, and listening carefully to what is really being said by the other person—rather than only hearing what you want to hear.

Flirting: The Final Word

Having fun, being a good conversationalist, building friendships, making people laugh—these are all part of normal social interaction. I enjoy them, my wife enjoys them, and lots of people we know enjoy them. In fact, these pleasures are available to everyone—whether they're married, in a serious relationship, dating, or unattached. But when the intent shifts from a desire to enjoy each other's company to an interest in developing an intimate relationship—then these behaviors cross the line into flirting. And flirting is something best left to, and enjoyed by, people who are still available.

19

The Big Day:
The Wedding

WEDDING. WHETHER YOU ARE a guest or a participant, we're talking about a very special occasion. Ideally, a wedding is a once-in-a-lifetime event. That makes this day incredibly important.

When you're the groom, you can multiply that last statement by a thousand. I'll talk about the groom's role a little later on. For the moment, however, let's focus on whenever you've been invited to a wedding as a guest. In everything you do—from responding to the invitation, to purchasing a wedding gift, to wearing the right clothes, to focusing on your date during the event—it's all about how you act and how your actions either make you look great or like a boor.

If you're attending the wedding with a date, your significant other, or your spouse, the stakes are even higher. My totally unscientific, personal observation is that women do a transference thing at weddings. It seems like during a wedding every woman—no matter what her relationship situation is—dreams of herself as a bride. And that fact raises the importance of weddings to all-time highs. You need to take this event very seriously and recognize just how important it is to the woman you are with, even if you'd rather be home mowing the grass.

The Guest: When You Are Invited

You can't miss it when it arrives in the mail—the handwritten address, the special shape of the envelope, the thick, high-quality paper. It's addressed to you personally.

Mr. John Sullivan
123 Main Street
Riverdale, CA 93656

Can You Bring an Uninvited Guest?

Now John faces an interesting problem: he and Marcia have been an item for about six months. Typically, when a couple is in a serious relationship but still living in two separate locations, each person will receive a wedding invitation. Since Marcia knows the betrothed couple as well, John wonders if maybe she received her own invitation. She hasn't said anything to him about it, so John calls up and asks her. Nope.

Can John go ahead and ask Marcia to go with him to the wedding?

No. No exceptions.

Here's why: in planning the wedding, the bride and groom carefully set the number of guests they are inviting. If just one person brought an uninvited guest, it wouldn't cause a problem. If five or ten or twenty people brought uninvited guests, it could play havoc with the table space, the amounts of food being served, the quantities of beverages being consumed, and ultimately the budget. So no exceptions: if Marcia isn't invited and John's invitation is addressed just to him, he shouldn't bring her, and he shouldn't ask if he can bring her.

On the other hand, there are a couple of scenarios in which Marcia could come along.

1. The bride might specifically invite both of them by including Marcia's name on the envelope, too. The following example shows how a wedding invitation is addressed to two people who live together, but who aren't married.

    Ms. Marcia Goodfellow
    Mr. John Sullivan
    123 Main Street
    Riverdale, CA 93656

Etiquette Imperative

....

If your children are not invited to a wedding and you can't get
childcare, *do not show up with your kids.*
If you do get stuck, make sure you let the bride know you can't attend,
and express your regrets with as much pleasantness as you can
muster: "I'm so sorry we can't come, but I simply can't find anyone to
take care of Joey and Sally."

....

2. The bride may have known John is in a serious relationship, but
   wasn't sure of the woman's name. In this case she addresses the
   invitation to:

Mr. John Sullivan and Guest
123 Main Street
Riverdale, CA 93656

Now, technically, when the invitation is worded this way, John doesn't
have to bring Marcia. He could bring his good friend Ralph or another
woman. In his response he should indicate the name of his guest, so the
bridal couple will know her name.

Kids

If the invitation lists your child(ren)'s names on the envelope, or if it
says, "Mr. and Mrs. John Sullivan and family," or if each child receives a
separate invitation, then the children are invited and may attend the wedding. If the invitation simply says, "Mr. and Mrs. John Sullivan," then the
kids are *not* invited. Don't bring them.

Exactly What Does RSVP Mean?

At the bottom of the invitation are four letters: RSVP. These letters
stand for *Répondez s'il vous plaît*, which is French for *Respond if you please*,
or, *Send an answer*. This imperative holds whether you're planning to
attend or not.

Usually, the invitation includes a preaddressed return envelope along
with a little card with a space for you to write your name and mark
"Accepts" or "Regrets." Use it.

If there is no response card, then write your response on a note card and send it. Wedding responses used to follow a highly formal structure that would send everyone running to *Emily Post's Etiquette* to make sure they were doing it the "right" way. In today's world, however, no matter how you word your response—as long as you aren't rude about it—your answer will be just fine.

Do I Have to Give a Wedding Gift?

Yes. This is true whether you attend or not.

If you're wondering what to give the happy couple, Dan and Jan have probably registered at several stores, and maybe even online as well. Phone Mrs. Nervous and ask her or someone else close to the couple. They expect these calls, so it's neither awkward nor embarrassing for you to ask them about this sort of information.

Remember, too, that just because Dan and Jan have registered somewhere, it *doesn't* mean you have to give them a gift from their registry list. One of the nicest gifts my wife and I received came from a good friend who gave us a case of very fine wine. Thank you, Chris!

Buy a gift prior to the wedding day. Have it delivered to the bride's home, to her parent's home, or to the couple's home if they already are living together.

What Should I Wear?

The clothing that men wear as guests at a wedding has undergone a marked transformation recently. A trend toward more informal dress has occurred, no question about it. But be careful about the definition of "less formal."

In planning what to wear for a wedding, you first need to be aware of

Tux or No Tux?

Traditionally, wedding invitations are not meant to specify the style of dress. Once in a while, however, the reception invitation may include the words "Black Tie," which indicate that you are *expected* to come dressed accordingly. Anything less would be disrespectful.

Etiquette Imperative

Wear a tie with a jacket or suit. This is a really important occasion for the bride, the groom, their families, and the person you are with. Honor them by wearing a shirt and tie with a jacket or with a suit.

the location of the event and the type of wedding: formal, semiformal, or informal. When in doubt, ask. My brother was married in a field behind our parents' house in Waterbury Center, Vermont. I don't think anyone was dressed in a suit, and a number of the men didn't wear a tie for the occasion, either. No one wore a T-shirt or jeans, though: every man was dressed very neatly in clean clothes with hair combed and faces shaved.

The three "acceptable" dress choices for male wedding guests all include some form of a tie. As I just pointed out, at my brother's wedding, some men came without a tie and still looked presentable. But from the point of view of what you *should* do—of what will make you look "sharp," and signal your respect for the specialness of the occasion—wear a tie. You can always remove your tie if the occasion warrants it.

And don't argue about it before the wedding. Just do it.

Here are the three options:

A TUXEDO. This attire is for the really formal wedding in the evening. If you don't own a tuxedo and it's expected, rent one. You wear it with a special shirt with French cuffs and a bow tie. It used to be only a black bow tie was acceptable, but today men wear a variety of colored and patterned bow ties with matching cummerbunds. (I have a great pink one that always elicits a few "oohs" and "ahs" from the ladies.) If the invitation indicates "Black Tie Optional," then you have the choice of wearing a suit or a tuxedo.

A DARK SUIT. This is acceptable at any wedding: day or evening, formal, semiformal, or informal. The only time you shouldn't wear a dark suit is when the invitation specifies Black Tie. Then, if you plan to attend, you really must wear a tuxedo. A dark suit is worn with a conservative (white, blue, pink, yellow, or striped) shirt and a tie.

A BLUE BLAZER OR DARK JACKET AND LIGHT PANTS (SUMMER ONLY) OR GRAY FLANNELS. Traditionally, the blazer or jacket was an option only at an informal, daytime wedding. Today, though, you'll see it worn interchangeably with the dark suit, especially when it's coupled with a pair of dark gray flannel pants. The only time I would *not* opt for a blue blazer or jacket would be at a formal daytime or evening wedding.

The Importance of Being Attentive

Weddings are incredibly special days, when the woman you're with really wants you to be near her, paying attention to her, making her the most important person in your life—just as the bride is the most honored person in the room on that particular day.

Forget the game on TV. Forget hanging out with the guys. Today, even though it's not your wedding, make it a special day for both of you by being her *prince*.

According to the Post Survey, the men who accomplish this are absolute heroes. Here are some of the things, our female respondents tell us, that heroes do at weddings:

> ➢ Act as if she is the most fascinating person in the world

> ➢ Show particular sensitivity to children, elderly people, and anyone feeling left out of the circle

> ➢ Talk to the other guests and be interested in what they have to say

> ➢ Have eyes only for her and make her feel like a very important part of his life

Etiquette Imperative

....

Dance!!!

When my daughters read the galleys for this book, they were emphatic about dancing. "Put lots of exclamation points after this word," they implored me. "Tell men how important dancing is to women." Now *they've* told you.

By the way, this holds for non-weddings, too. Even on your average night out, dance with your date. It's a sure bet to make her happy.

....

➤ Whisper sweet things in her ear when other people are around

➤ Include her in conversations with others she may not know

➤ Make a concerted effort to socialize

Reread this list and memorize it. If you do these things, you'll make this day very memorable for your date. And that's a very good thing for everyone.

When to Leave

Eating fast and then leaving immediately doesn't cut it at weddings. In fact, "cutting it" is the signal for when it's okay to leave—after the cutting of the cake, that is.

Thank You

As always, whenever you are a guest, before you leave you must be sure to thank the hosts. Make a point of seeking out the bride and groom (if they haven't left already) as well as the bride's parents and the groom's parents. Thank all of them for including you at this wonderful event.

Then, the next day, sit down and write each of them a thank-you note. Two or three sentences is fine. Technically, this note is optional, but it is an incredibly nice thing to do.

Getting Engaged

There are as many different ways of getting engaged as there are stars in the sky. There's really only one piece of advice I can give you on this point: it's a big moment and a big commitment, so be sure of what you're doing. Beyond that, how you pop the question is up to you. Just remember: the more complex a plan you concoct, the more chance there is for something to go wrong.

As for me, I had no plan. My wife and I got engaged in a Volkswagen Beetle at a gas station in Caldwell, New Jersey. It was January, and we had just finished visiting her parents.

"Their schedule sure is filling up fast," I said to my future wife. In my usual clueless way, I'd simply assumed we were getting married. "If we're going to get married this summer, maybe we should tell them now." And suddenly we both realized that we'd just crossed the Rubicon. (That's the

"Should I Ask Her Dad for Permission?"

In the Post Survey, we asked: *Should* the man ask her parents for permission? A surprising 56 percent said, "Yes."

In the final analysis, individual circumstances will determine whether you should ask permission, either alone or with your intended, or if you should simply announce your plans together. Be respectful of the culture and traditions of your future wife's family. This will help you decide on the most appropriate course of action. (I can't help wondering if the men in my daughters' lives will read this!)

river Caesar forded on his march to Rome. After crossing it, there was no turning back.)

No kneeling, no ring. I know it doesn't sound very romantic, and it wasn't—but the marriage has lasted thirty years, so go figure.

Recently, my nephew showed real class and imagination. As he and his intended walked across the Brooklyn Bridge, he stopped, went down on bended knee, and proposed to her. Personally, I would have tied some dental floss to the ring and held on to the other end for dear life, just in case the ring slipped.

The Bachelor Party

The bachelor party is one of those infamous anachronisms for which more legend has been created than facts can attest to. Having one is entirely optional. Contrary to popular opinion, a bachelor party is *not* an opportunity for the groom-to-be to sow one final bunch of wild oats before he's tied down for good. It *is* an opportunity for the groom and his close friends to spend some quality time together, and perhaps escape the craziness of the final wedding preparations for a few hours.

Be creative when planning this gathering of men. When my nephew recently got married, as the best man his older brother arranged a bachelor outing consisting of a canoe trip down the Connecticut River along the Vermont/New Hampshire border. He rented canoes and sleeping gear, and laid in an abundance of supplies. They had a great and memorable time. And that's what it's all about.

The Groom's Big Day

Today's Groom

Today's groom often participates to a much greater degree than grooms of the past. Most important, brides and grooms are more often financially responsible for the wedding. The groom often takes a full partner's role in planning the size and type of wedding. He spends time with the bride making selections for gift registries. He shares in the task of writing thank-you notes. He attends meetings with caterers and other service providers. And he helps determine the invitation list.

My mother-in-law-to-be gave me just one task at our wedding: be at the church on time.

I was.

The Receiving Line

After making sure you're actually present for the ceremony, your next duty will be to stand in the receiving line if there is one. Frankly, I don't remember doing this—but my wife assures me I was there, and has the photos to prove it. It's an opportunity for her family's friends and relatives to meet you, and for your family's friends and relatives to wish you well.

Smearing Cake in Your Bride's Face

Don't do it.

Toasts

One of the most terrifying ordeals any man will face is standing up in front of a crowd and giving a toast. Often this high-pressure moment occurs after the *toaster* is already *toasted*. Mix a person's natural nervousness with some alcohol and an unplanned toast, and you have a recipe for disaster. Since you can't do much about the nervousness, and since I'm not going to tell you to hold off on all champagne until after the toasts, you've got only one recourse: write down your toast on paper a couple of days ahead of time, and then practice it a few times—out loud. Remember to bring the paper with you.

Here are a few other tips:

> Keep your toast short. Short is very good from everyone's point of view.

> Always start by thanking everyone for coming. You can even make a special point of thanking the people who came from farthest away.

> Thank her parents. Tell them how happy you are to be part of their family.

> Thank your parents.

> And then honor your bride.

That's it—your official duties are done. Enjoy the evening with your bride. Go with her to visit with the guests. Then dance the night away, at least until it's time to leave.

The Best Man

Ideally, the best man is supposed to be the stable, level-headed rock on whom the groom—who is expected to be totally frazzled on the day of his wedding, and usually is—can rely to help him get ready and get to the church on time. (I said "ideally." In practice, I know of some best men who needed more help than the groom did.)

Besides arranging the bachelor party (see above), the best man is also responsible for making sure the wedding rings make it to the altar. He should either give the wedding rings to the ring bearer just before the ceremony, or bring the rings up to the altar himself, where, at the appropriate time, he hands them to the person performing the ceremony.

Whatever else you do as best man—<u>don't forget the rings</u>.

Another major responsibility of the best man is to toast the bride and groom at the reception. The toast should be an expression of good wishes to the happy couple, of thanks to the groom for being such a great friend, and of joy at the fact that the groom has found such a fantastic person to share his life with. Save your wild stories of the past for the occasional "guys' night."

When You're an Usher

As one of the ushers, you may be invited to a couple of pre-wedding parties. For the big event itself, you'll be asked to dress in specific clothes. Often this involves renting a tuxedo. If so, the groom will let you know exactly what you need to rent. In addition to the wedding gift, you'll also probably be asked to chip in on an ushers' present. Your other responsibilities include escorting women to their seats at the wedding ceremony, and being prepared to run any last-minute errands for the bride or groom. At the reception, make sure that you dance with the mothers of the bride and the groom, as well as with the maid of honor and the bridesmaids, and keep an eye out to make sure the bridesmaids are having a great time.

Finally—have a great time yourself!

....

PART THREE

On the Job

20

·······································

Top Three Issues
for Work Life

NOW THAT YOU'RE AN expert on situations involving daily life and the social world, prepare to move back to square one—because the work world presents a completely different set of etiquette problems, which are critically important to your welfare and your future. How you handle yourself on the job will have a major impact not only on your own performance, but also on the morale and productivity of your colleagues and the trajectory of your career. When you treat your co-workers with consideration and respect, you are helping your business become a happier and more efficient enterprise. Fail to show consideration, on the other hand, and you become a business liability.

I own an advertising agency, and whenever I hire someone, I tell that person right up front that I have three inviolable rules, which if broken will lead to dismissal. Two of these rules have to do with productivity.

Rule Number Three is the "people rule": *You must be able to get along with the other people in the office.* If you can't, then I'll be forced to choose between who can stay and who has to go—and you might not like my choice.

This third rule illuminates the key differences between your work life and your nonwork life. In the business world, no matter what your job, you are going to have to:

> ➤ Work with people with whom you otherwise might not choose to associate

> ➤ Listen and take instruction or guidance from someone with whom you don't always agree

> ➤ Do things in a certain way, even if you don't always believe this is the best way to do them

Suppose that you work at my advertising agency, and you don't like a certain co-worker very much, or you think the sales rep for one of our suppliers is an idiot, or you cringe every time you have to do work for a particular client. From your perspective, your behavior toward these people is understandable and defensible: your cold-shoulder, abrupt, and uncommunicative treatment of your fellow employee is your way of saying, "Stay out of my space—I may have to work here but I don't have to deal with you"; your superior attitude toward the supplier arises from your impatience at his plodding way of reviewing every purchase request; and your readiness to argue over every question, comment, or objection the client makes is your way of emphasizing that your solutions are the "right" ones.

From *my* perspective, however, your behavior tells a very different story: your rudeness toward your co-worker is resulting in lost productivity for both of you; your superior attitude toward the supplier is causing him *not* to go the extra mile for our company; and your ongoing arguments with our client are the first step on the road to losing him as a client.

I need people who know how to get along with and bring out the best in other people, despite any differences they may have—people who know how to listen and learn, and who are able to put aside their personal likes or dislikes and pull together to produce the finest possible work. In short: *businesses need people who know how to <u>build</u> relationships—not tear them down.*

The work world revolves around relationships. Your work skills may get you in the door to sit for a job interview or make a sales pitch. But it's your *people skills*—your ability to connect with an interviewer, or a prospective buyer, or your boss or your co-workers—that will drive your success.

The Two Biggest Issues in Work Life

Given what we were just talking about, it won't surprise you to learn that the two most annoying work-related behaviors of men relate directly to the aforementioned Rule Number Three. The first involves men who put their co-workers down, and the second has to do with men who act superior to their colleagues. These behaviors can often be traced to the fact the worker in question simply "doesn't like" the co-worker he is putting down—but whatever the reason, these attitudes are a mistake. Whenever you put other people down, or act as if you're "better than" they are, you can't avoid being rude to them in the process.

Consequences of Rudeness in the Workplace

A recent survey on rudeness in the workplace discovered that among those people who reported they were victims of rude behavior on the job, 22 percent consciously decreased their work effort, and 12 percent (one out of every eight people) actually left their jobs because of the rude behavior.

No business owner—no matter how successful—can afford to lose a valued employee for such a preventable reason. Training a new person costs time and money, and every dollar of this cost comes out of profits.

Negative Behavior #1: Putting People Down

When you put other people down, you are directly assaulting their sense of themselves by demeaning them, belittling them, and trying to tear down their self-esteem and belief in their own value. It doesn't matter whether you do these things intentionally or not: if you can see yourself in any of the behaviors I'm about to describe, you need to think long and hard about what that behavior says about you—and about how you can start breaking the habit of using that behavior.

> ➤ Do you try to dominate others?

> ➤ Do you shout and bully?

> ➤ Do you use false terms of endearment?

> ➤ Do you flirt on the job?

> ➤ Do you interrupt colleagues?

> ➤ Do you ogle and stare at attractive co-workers?

Negative Behavior #2: A Superior Attitude

Acting superior is the flip side of putting down or belittling. When you demean someone, the focus of the behavior is on the person who is being put down. When your behavior says, "I think I'm better than you and/or more important than you," then the focus is on you—the person who is acting in a superior way.

Sometimes a superior attitude will be overt and very obvious. Other times it may be more subtle, but just as destructive. Again, if you recognize yourself in any of the following behaviors, it's time for a little soul-searching:

➤ Are you macho?

➤ Do you act power hungry?

➤ Are you a know-it-all?

➤ Do you act like you own the place?

➤ Do you assume that because a person has a "lesser" position, they're not as smart as you?

➤ Are you late?

➤ Do you fail to listen carefully?

➤ Are you "one of the boys"?

➤ Do you refuse to do your share?

Lack of Manners—
The Third Annoying Office Behavior

While manners aren't as big an issue as demeaning behavior and a superior attitude, be assured that your co-workers *will* take notice when good manners are lacking.

At the Emily Post Institute, we've gotten some astonishing stories about people's poor manners, such as the men (there seem to be a number of them out there) who like to sit at their cubicle desks, take off their shoes and socks, and start clipping their toenails. Or the worker who attended a mandatory seminar and sat in the back of the room reading the newspaper the whole time. Or the sales associate who was riding in an elevator full of people following a sales call, and turned to his supervisor and started talking about the deal they just negotiated. Or the group of male employees who wanted to know if it was really necessary to leave the toilet seat down in a unisex bathroom.

The interesting thing about manners in the workplace is that often problems center on the little things rather than major faux pas. The trouble is the little things add up. Flash points that got the most complaints in the Post Survey included sloppy table manners, lousy phone and e-mail etiquette, not making introductions properly, simple failure to say "please" or "thank you," not holding doors for women, bad hygiene, and inappropriate clothing.

Things Men Do Well in Work Life

On the positive side, people have great respect for co-workers and business colleagues who treat them as equals, listen to them, praise them when they deserve it, are polite, and get the job done. If you do these things consistently and sincerely, you'll find these behaviors will make a real difference in the quality of your business relationships.

These behaviors really come down to treating your business associates with consideration, respect, and honesty. And that's exactly what your co-workers want. In fact, they've said so, in survey after survey. A recent survey of six thousand workers asked which non-monetary benefits mattered most to them. The first three had to do with the quality of their work environment, and how they were treated by their colleagues.

71 percent Enjoyable co-workers

68 percent A pleasant work environment

62 percent An understanding boss

Enjoyable co-workers? A pleasant work environment? An understanding boss? These aspects of a job matter nowadays. If the major part of your waking life is going to be spent at work, then surely you want to spend that time with people you can get along with, in a reasonably enjoyable and positive environment. People who contribute to this kind of positive work environment will prosper, while people who drag the environment down are going to suffer the consequences.

21

Five Cardinal Rules for Your Job Interview

1. Don't Be Late

Mr. Job Applicant—Come—Lately asked, "I was twenty minutes late for one job interview, but I was only *five* minutes late for another. I didn't get either job, and I think it was because I was late. Is this fair?"

"Five minutes, one minute, it doesn't matter. No job. No excuses, no exceptions," I answered firmly.

"Even just *five* minutes late?"

"That's just the way it is: if you're late for the interview, don't expect to be offered the job."

Above all others, there is one inviolable rule when interviewing for a job: *be there on time.* Your arrival is your first opportunity to make a good impression on your prospective employers. If you keep your interviewer waiting even a minute or two, you'll most likely never recover from the bad impression you've made.

Lateness is *never* a mark of importance. Rather, it is a mark of rudeness, arrogance, or disorganization—personality traits you certainly don't want people to associate with you. Any time you're late, whether you are a job applicant or a CEO, whether it involves work or play, you're being disrespectful of the people you're supposed to be meeting.

Here's how to avoid the problem: go to the site a day or two before the interview. Learn how long the trip will take. Then factor in some extra time just to be on the safe side. If there is no security checkpoint, go into the business itself, introduce yourself to the receptionist. That way you'll know exactly where the office is. This also gives you a chance to check out what people are wearing in the office, so that you can be sure you're dressed appropriately for the interview. If there is a security checkpoint, then simply observe the dress of the people entering the premises (see Job Interview Tip #3: Dress One Notch Up).

On the day of the interview, plan to get there five to ten minutes ahead of time. If you arrive really early, you can always stop at a diner down the street for a cup of coffee. In a worst-case scenario when you find yourself stuck on a commuter train that has stalled between stations or at a dead standstill in a monumental traffic jam, this is the perfect time to use your cell phone. Call and explain the circumstances that have made you unavoidably delayed. Apologize profusely, give them an estimate of when you will arrive, and ask if they would prefer to reschedule. If you're lucky, you may salvage the situation.

2. Be Prepared

The job interview is not about your *job* skills; it is about your *personal* skills. Your job skills are what got you in the door—you wouldn't even be there if the company didn't think you had the skills and the potential to do the job. What really makes the difference is how well you connect with the interviewer(s). To make that connection, you'll need to draw on your full array of personal skills, including:

➤ How you stand, sit, dress, talk, listen, and respond to the interviewer

➤ How confident you are

➤ How knowledgeable you are about the company

➤ How comfortable you are talking about yourself

A Job Interview Is a Two-Way Street

Remember, a job interview is a two-way street: not only is it an opportunity for a company to learn what type of person *you* are and whether they think you'll fit their corporate culture—but it's also an opportunity for you to learn if *they* are a good fit for your needs. Ask yourself if the interviewer is the type of person you'd really like to work for. The same goes for any other people you meet during the interview. Consider carefully, too, if the job tasks they've defined for you are tasks you are interested in doing.

> ➤ How well you project an image that matches the type of person the company is searching for

Getting ready for a job interview is like prepping for an exam. Learn everything you can about the company you are interviewing with. Look them up on the Internet—these days, they will almost surely have a web site. If they don't, ask them why not at the point when they inquire if you have any questions. Just by asking this question, you're showing you've been doing research on them (always a good thing to convey), and you'll also show them that you are computer literate.

3. Dress One Notch Up

There are very few hard and fast, "do it this way" rules in this book.

This is one of them.

Okay, so you were working for a dot.com company where the dress code embraced T-shirts, jeans, and no socks. But those days are over, and now you're applying for a job at an insurance agency.

Different culture. New rules. *Their* rules. So be sure you dress for the

What *Not* to Ask

The initial job interview is *not* the time to ask how many vacation days you get, what kind of benefits are offered, and how many holidays you get. The time to ask these types of questions and negotiate a salary is after you've already been offered the job and are deciding whether or not to accept the offer.

part. In fact, for the job interview, you should always dress just a little sharper than the norm for that corporate culture. If the guys typically wear slacks and a shirt but no tie, you should wear a coat and tie. If they are wearing sports jackets and ties, wear a suit. The idea is to always dress one notch up.

4. Smile, Speak Clearly, and Look Your Interviewer in the Eye

People who smile exude confidence. If you can show your interviewer that you are confident (but not cocky), you will also be showing him or her that you have the ability to represent the company as a confident, can-do person. So *smile*. Not a big crazy grin, just a relaxed, confident smile.

Speaking clearly is also vital. If the person conducting the interview can't understand you, then he/she will assume that co-workers, prospects, clients, suppliers, and the general public won't be able to understand you either. Translation: no job.

Finally comes the importance of looking people in the eye. I'm disconcerted when I interview someone who can't meet my eyes. Their gaze wanders to the left, to the right, to their lap, their fingers, anywhere but at me. Again: no job.

Review the body language tips in chapter 23 to make sure you present the best image possible.

5. Thank Them Twice

The first thank-you should come at the end of the interview. When the interview is finished, stand and shake hands with each person in the meeting. While shaking hands, look that person in the eye and thank him/her simply and directly. For example, you might say: "Thank you for the opportunity to interview for the job. I've enjoyed meeting you and am looking forward to hearing from you soon."

When you get home that evening, type a thank-you note, essentially repeating what you said in person. An hour or so later reread it. Look for any possible errors in punctuation, grammar, word usage, spelling, names, and titles. Then ask a roommate, spouse, significant other, friend, parent, or other relative—anyone you trust—to read it for you as well. Make sure it is mistake free.

Thank-You Note Tips

This is your final opportunity to show your prospective employer how well you communicate.

➤ Since this is a business communication, you should type it.

➤ Keep it short—no more than one page.

➤ You don't need to restate your qualifications in the letter. The company already has your résumé and your application.

➤ If anything came up in the interview that focused on a particular strength you have, you can reiterate it here. Example: "During the interview you mentioned the importance of building a presence on the Web. I had the opportunity to help build the Youth Corps web site last summer. I have checked with Tom Miller, the director, and he would be happy to talk with you about my work on the Youth Corps site. His number is 802-555-1221."

➤ End on a positive note: "Thank you for your time and interest. I look forward to the possibility of joining your staff."

➤ Send your thank-you note by "snail mail"—through the postal system with a stamp on it. This is *not* the time for an e-mailed thank-you.

Then, and only then, print out a final version on your personal stationery and put your thank-you note into a matching envelope, place a stamp on it (don't use a postage meter), and deposit it in the mail.

Five Interview Questions You Should Be Prepared to Answer

Setting aside some time in advance to practice your answers to the usual questions you can expect in a job interview will give you an edge of confidence during the interview itself. This confidence will translate into a comfortable, positive attitude, which will reflect well on you and could even prove to be the decisive factor in your getting the job. The best way to practice is to say your answers out loud in a normal tone of voice. So here we go.

WHY DO YOU WANT A NEW JOB? Stay positive when answering this question. This isn't the time to denigrate your current employer or co-workers. Indicate that you're ready for a new challenge and that you believe this position will give you that opportunity.

WHAT DO YOU KNOW ABOUT OUR COMPANY AND WHY DO YOU WANT A POSITION WITH US? Here's where your preparation pays off. You can reiterate your desire for a new challenge and go on to mention specific products or services the company offers and how your previous experience matches these products and services. This question also gives you an opportunity to indicate that you have heard good comments about the company during your networking.

WHAT ARE YOUR STRENGTHS? Rather than rattling off a list of values, it's better to provide a few concrete examples of your positive skills at work. Relate a specific example from your current job: "I'm good at stepping up to the plate when a job needs doing. I filled in for my manager when he was out sick for two weeks. I really enjoyed the responsibility and the challenge of the task."

WHAT WAS THE HARDEST THING YOU FACED IN A PREVIOUS JOB? You can't answer this question if you are not prepared. This is *not* the time to hash over a disaster that you were part of. Instead, describe a tough situation that you were instrumental in resolving.

TELL ME ABOUT YOURSELF. This is your opportunity to highlight the skills you think will be most valuable to the company. The more you understand about the prospective job and the company before you interview, the better you can equate your skills and capabilities with the company's needs.

Five Questions to Ask During an Interview

WHICH OF THE JOB'S RESPONSIBILITIES ARE THE MOST IMPORTANT ONES? So far you've only seen a written description of the job responsibilities. As the interviewer expands on those responsibilities, you can use this new information to point out how your qualifications match the key job responsibilities he/she is outlining. You'll also gain valuable information that can help you decide whether this job is really one you *want*, should it be offered to you.

COULD WE TAKE A FEW MINUTES TO REVIEW MY RÉSUMÉ? An astonishing number of interviewers will not have reviewed your résumé. Whether that's the case or not, use this question as an opening to review the highlights of your résumé that best fit the job you're applying for.

WHAT DOES THE INTERVIEWER CONSIDER TO BE THE STRENGTHS OF THE COMPANY? The interviewer's response is not the point here. By asking the interviewer for his/her opinion, you will then have a chance to respond with comments that show your own knowledge of the company.

WHAT ARE THE MAIN PROBLEMS FACING THE STAFF TODAY? Listen carefully to the response—then go on to compare your talents and skills as they relate to the challenges outlined by your interviewer. The idea is to position yourself as someone who can come in and have an immediate, positive impact.

HOW WOULD YOU DESCRIBE THE SUCCESSFUL CANDIDATE FOR THIS JOB? This question lets you align your capabilities to what the company is seeking. Listen carefully to the points the interviewer raises—then respond point by point. By doing this, not only are you addressing the company's needs, but you're also showing the interviewer that you can listen effectively.

22

Building Better
Relationships

EMILY POST ALWAYS MADE it quite clear that the essence of etiquette was about building the best possible relationships with everyone in your life. In her first book on manners, *Etiquette,* published in 1922,
Emily Post noted that some people did not believe etiquette was important in business—and then cautioned her readers not to toss this valuable
business tool aside:

> A certain rich man whose appointment to a foreign post of impor-
> tance was about to be ratified, came into the corridor of a Wash-
> ington hotel and stopped to speak with a lady for a few moments.
> During the whole conversation he kept his hat on his head and a
> cigar in the corner of his mouth. It happened that the lady was the
> wife of a prominent senator, and she lost no time in reporting
> the incident to her husband, who in turn brought the matter to the
> attention of certain of his colleagues with the result that the
> appointment did not go through.

People watch how other people conduct themselves in their various
relationships. We all get judged by our "people skills" as well as our "job

skills," and in business the final choice often comes down to this "people skills" judgment.

People skills are a balance of knowledge of manners and the ability to use the principles to resolve etiquette issues. Emily also recognized the importance of mastering the *principles* of etiquette rather than just mastering a superficial display of manners and used no less a gentleman than Abraham Lincoln as her prime example:

> Because Lincoln's etiquette was self-taught he was no less masterly for that! Whether he happened to know a lot of trifling details of pseudo etiquette matters not in the least. Awkward he may have been, but the essence of him was courtesy—unfailing courtesy.

Courtesy is a term that embodies the three principles of etiquette: consideration, respect, and honesty. Mastering the principles of etiquette means using these principles to enhance interactions and to build the most positive, successful relationships possible. At all times, *positive relationships are the ultimate goal*. The more successful you are at building such relationships, the more you'll succeed at your work.

Understanding How to Build Relationships

If I simply challenged you to go out and start building better relationships, you'd probably roll your eyes and stop reading this book on the spot. But this goal becomes much more attainable when you stop to consider that there are really only three factors that affect a relationship: actions, words, and appearance. Focus on improving these three areas, and good relationships will naturally follow.

Changing Your Actions, Words, and Appearance for the Better

Once you break down your "relationship issues" into these three areas—actions, words, and appearance—you'll find it much easier to pinpoint specific things you can do to improve your relationships.

If you can identify specific ways in which your actions, words, or appearance may be causing problems for your co-workers, and then take concrete steps to change this behavior, you'll be well on the way to building better, more successful relationships in the future.

Words Matter

....

What you choose to say and how you say it will be remembered by other people and will have a profound influence on how they view you.

The most obvious negative example of this is the way people—especially young people, it seems to me—litter their speech with the "f-word" these days. Their choice of language leaves me profoundly unimpressed: they're certainly not convincing me that they're "grown up"; and if they think the shock value of this word is going to get me to pay attention to them, they should realize that the "f-word" lost its shock value long ago. Not only am I *not* going to pay special attention to them because they use that word, but it may well cause me to tune them out.

Obscenity and coarse language have no place in business; they do nothing to enhance communication, and do everything to enhance your image as a person with a foul mouth. But you can also ruffle feathers simply by using words that might be normal for you, but which are offensive to someone else.

....

Here are some of the most common work-related "negative behaviors," along with suggestions on how to change them for the better. These annoying behaviors tear down relationships, cause hard feelings, and, if left unaddressed, can ultimately lead to reduced productivity, lost profits, and high employee turnover.

Inappropriate Touching

Tom, Jane's boss, walks into her cubicle to speak with her about a new assignment. As the conversation ends, Tom stands and reaches forward with his left hand. "Thanks for taking on this assignment. I really appreciate it," he says, and gently squeezes her arm.

It's just a friendly touch—nothing more. In Tom's eyes, his gesture is simply an attempt on his part to show that he truly appreciates the effort Jane is making.

Jane, however, sees it another way. To Jane, Tom's arm squeeze is just plain weird. "Why did he do that?" she thinks to herself. "I've never seen him touch a male employee, other than to shake his hand. Why didn't he just shake *my* hand? What's going on here? Is he making a pass at me? Is there more to this than he's letting on?"

WHAT TO DO: Something as simple as touching a woman can lead to major interpersonal problems, not to mention a lawsuit. If you feel you want to connect with a colleague in a physical way, *reach out and offer to shake hands* as you thank him or her for taking on the assignment. Stay away from all other forms of touching in the workplace.

Terms of Endearment

"Honey," "darling," "babe"—there are loads of these terms. The speaker who uses these endearments may think he's just being friendly. But to the co-worker who is their recipient, these terms can come across as depersonalizing, inappropriately informal or forward, or even a form of unacceptable flirting.

Bob gets up to leave Jane's office. No touching, he reminds himself. Instead, he says, "Thanks, sweetie."

"Sweetie?" Jane thinks to herself, as she stares at his receding back. "I'm not your 'sweetie'—I'm *Jane*. J-A-N-E."

WHAT TO DO: If you wouldn't use a certain word when you're addressing a male co-worker, don't use it when you're talking to a woman, either. As a general rule, avoid all terms of endearment in the workplace. People have names. Use them. You won't go wrong.

Bullying

Bullying is a classic "ends-justify-the-means" action. Bullying is a way of coercing people to do things they don't want to do: "Come on, Jack—let's take the company car. What are you, a wus? No one will ever know!"

In this bully's mind, the "ends" of going out to lunch, rather than eating at the company cafeteria, clearly justify the "means" of getting Jack to disobey company regulations. In today's work world, bullying rarely if ever accomplishes its intended goal.

WHAT TO DO: Bullying is unacceptable, period—whether it involves coercing a co-worker to borrow a company car for personal business, or demanding that a colleague use illegal accounting practices to cover up a billion-dollar loss. Follow the rules, and let those around you know that you expect them to do the same.

Swearing, Shouting, and Using Coarse Language

It doesn't matter whether or not the phrase is offensive to *you*—what matters is if it is offensive to someone else with whom you're interacting.

WHAT TO DO: Whenever I speak with people, I try to take into account their different backgrounds and cultures, as well as the geographic regions they hail from. I need to ensure that my word choice doesn't get in the way of my goal—which is to deliver my message effectively, and build the best relationship possible with my audience.

Being Domineering

You can be domineering with your words, your actions, or your appearance. When the intent of your words is to put down the other person rather than discuss the issue at hand ("You don't know what you are talking about!" "How could you say something so stupid?"), you've crossed the line from arguing to being domineering.

The tone in which you deliver your words—especially if you shout—can be just as domineering as the words you use. Finally, body language can be incredibly intimidating and domineering as well—particularly if it involves standing over or standing very close to another person.

WHAT TO DO: When discussing a problem with a co-worker or business associate, outline the problem in a neutral, nonpersonal way, using words that *critique* rather than words that *criticize*. Stay calm and keep your voice under control, your tone modulated and steady. Anytime your voice betrays anger or frustration, the person you're speaking with will inevitably begin reacting to your emotional state, rather than to the issue at hand. Be cognizant of your body language, as well: it won't help to control your tone of voice if you're "shouting" with your body.

Ogling

"I *try* not to stare," you protest—"but sometimes she wears clothes that are designed more to catch a man's eye than to do work in."

I know it can be hard, especially when a particularly good-looking woman is in the room. And some of those outfits *are* eye-catching. But that doesn't change the fact that staring or ogling is inappropriate behavior in the workplace.

WHAT TO DO: It may be that the good-looking colleague doesn't care that she's crossed the line—but the other people in the room (both men and women alike) *will* care. They expect you and everyone else in the room to be focused on the job at hand and to be able to concentrate even if there is a distraction. Your attention needs to be on the information and knowledge each person brings to the task, and *not* on their physical attributes. When you're at work, learn to focus on work. Save the looking for after hours.

Ignoring Other People's Opinions

All too often, when I talk with business people around the country, I hear complaints about men failing to listen, or men ignoring other people's opinions, or men not giving credit when credit is due. In the "team environment" of today's corporations, this sort of behavior has become more noticeable and disruptive than ever before. Building strong, cohesive teams is an integral part of business today.

This means learning to function within a collaborative team environment, rather than maintaining a competitive, "doing-my-thing-alone" attitude. For example, let's say the software team at xyz.com has been asked to develop a new computer game. The development process is complex, and focus is critical to the team's success—but if team members are distracted by feelings of frustration over the attitudes of other team members, they won't be able to focus properly. When Jill writes a weekly report that makes it sound like the latest innovation is her idea alone, the other team members become resentful and suspicious of Jill—("I'll bet she's angling for a promotion")—and less cooperative.

WHAT TO DO: Listen carefully to what others are saying—and show that you're listening by asking probing questions or building on their train of thought. Acknowledge others when they make a contribution: "Great concept, Jill. What can we do to enhance it further? Ideas anyone?" This will keep the focus on the work, and not on personal slights.

Interrupting

Interrupting is cutting another person off at the knees, plain and simple. It says to the other person: "Sorry, Jack, but whatever you have to say isn't worth the time it takes to say it."

WHAT TO DO: Start listening. Stop interrupting.

Stop Demeaning, and Drop the Superior Attitude

When we asked respondents to name the most annoying things men did on the job, two categories dominated the list: *demeaning behavior*, and *a superior attitude*. Together, these two accounted for two-thirds of all "annoying behaviors" cited.

Demeaning behavior of one kind or another was mentioned in 35 percent of the responses—more than one out of every three. This included such things as domineering behavior, shouting or bullying, and interrupting.

Another 31 percent of the responses complained about co-workers who acted as if they were better than everyone else. Our respondents detailed example after example: there was John, who always lets everyone in the office know that there's no problem he can't solve, and that he's always informed of every decision before anyone else. Or Jason, always ready to take on any task—and take all the credit for any work the team does. Or Jim, who starts acting like *he's* running the show whenever the boss is away.

Choosing to Get Along

One fact that differentiates work life from daily and social life is that you don't get to choose your work colleagues. They come with the job—which means that to succeed at your job, you have to get along with people you might otherwise choose not to associate with.

This challenge is especially great at the start of any new job. Whenever you put a man into a strange environment, such as a new workplace, there's a natural tendency for him to switch into a defensive, competitive mode. Add to the mix some people that the man doesn't "take to" or whom he feels uncomfortable around, and his defensiveness can shift over all too easily into demeaning actions and/or a superior attitude—the two leading sources of workplace friction.

Understandable? Possibly. Defensible? No.

Be aware that whenever you enter a new work environment, your natural defenses are automatically going to kick in at first. To overcome this and immediately begin forging positive new relationships . . .

> Focus on being a member of the team

> Listen—*really* listen—to what your co-workers are saying

➤ Concentrate on doing the tasks that your education and experience have prepared you to do

➤ Work on finding value in your colleagues and learning from them

And finally, like Lincoln, let the essence of you be courtesy—unfailing courtesy.

23

Office Communications

IF YOU LEARN ONLY one lesson from this chapter, let it be this: *You can't take back your communications.*

"I didn't say that."

(Yes, you did.)

"I didn't mean that."

(It's what they heard.)

"Please ignore my previous communication."

(Right!)

Whether you say it or you write it, once a message has been sent, it becomes a reflection of who you are. Jumbled, incoherent thoughts and rambling communications make you appear disorganized and ignorant. Typos, poor grammar, or embarrassing word choices make you look sloppy, imprecise, and foolish. The recipient's feelings of annoyance, frustration, or derision suddenly become the focus, rather than the message you really intended to communicate.

No matter what form of communication you use—face-to-face conversation, e-mail, memo, letter, fax, or telephone—if you satisfy the following four criteria, people will focus on your content and not your inadequacies:

➤ Is it clear? (Have you said what you intended to say?)

➤ Is it unified? (Have you stuck to your point?)

➤ Is it coherent? (Will the communication make sense to the recipient?)

➤ Is it focused? (Could you have said your piece more succinctly or written it more concisely?)

Unfortunately, with the business world in hyper-drive these days, the clarity, conciseness, unity, and coherence of corporate communications seem to be diminishing. Here is a review of the different mediums used to communicate in today's fast-paced business world, and some tips on how to make the most of them.

Face-to-Face

In some ways, face-to-face communications are the most difficult of all. When you're talking face-to-face, people can hear you, see you, and smell you. There's a lot that can go wrong, and many ways to screw up. You've got to consider tone and quality of voice, grammar and word choice, pronunciation, clarity, and body language.

Case in point: Bob is slated to give a major presentation to his company's board of directors. This is it—his chance to shine, or to crash and burn. He's run through his PowerPoint presentation a dozen times already to make sure that the equipment operates without a hitch. But he should also make a point-by-point check of his *own* equipment.

➤ Is his voice confident and clear or does it quaver from nervousness?

➤ Does he speak concisely or does he tend to repeat himself three times every time he makes a point?

➤ Does he speak at a regular pace or does he race through his presentation at ninety miles per hour?

➤ Is he comfortable with the appropriate lingo or does he mispronounce words?

➤ Does he move around the room as he talks or does he grip the podium like a vise?

➢ Does he engage members of the audience with his eyes and with hand and arm gestures, or does he stand like a statue, eyes fixed on his notes?

➢ Is he dressed appropriately for the occasion? (I once forgot my belt and had to keep my jacket buttoned throughout the presentation.)

Here are some pointers on how to make your face-to-face communications more effective:

Speaking Volume

Shouting your words won't give your argument more strength. Talk in a conversational tone. If you're going to use a microphone for a presentation, practice with one ahead of time to give yourself a chance to get used to hearing your own voice amplified.

Tone of Voice

There's nothing more conducive to putting your audience to sleep than speaking in a monotone. Also, speaking in an animated voice helps the listener discern the important parts of what you are saying. Your tone of voice can either imply "I don't give a hoot about what I'm talking about," or it can say to your audience, "This is really important—listen up."

Rate of Speech

Ideally, when speaking to a group, you should talk at the same speed you would use when talking with a friend.

Accent

Normally, a slight accent isn't a problem. But if your accent is so thick and heavy that people have to strain to understand what you are saying, then you need to work on reducing it.

Body Language

How you look is just as important as what you have to say. Through your posture, you can either engage the person you are talking with or you can reject him or her completely. Of course, one's posture or action alone doesn't necessarily convey an attitude. On its own, the act of crossing your arms and leaning back might not mean anything. But couple it with some curt questions, a scowling face, or tightly pursed lips, and you may have good reason to believe the other person is not particularly receptive to your comments.

The eyes are powerful communicators, as well. If you avoid looking someone in the eyes, it may indicate that you feel awkward about his presence or uncomfortable about what he is saying. If you stare too long into someone's eyes, you may be subtly challenging her authority.

Slouching conveys an impression of laziness or not caring.

The hands-in-pockets posture is more casual, while keeping your hands out of your pockets, perhaps even clasped behind you, projects a more authoritative image.

Finally, jiggling a foot or knee while sitting can communicate a sense of exasperation, impatience, anxiety, or boredom to the person with whom you are talking.

Grammar Quiz

Learning proper grammar is essential if you want to communicate your ideas clearly and effectively. Here's a short quiz: if you miss any of these questions, you might want to consider taking a course in grammar and expository writing. You can also find answers to many grammar questions in *The Elements of Style* by William Strunk Jr., E. B. White, and Roger Angell.

SUBJECT/OBJECT (1)

A. When your boss asks, "Who's going to the meeting?" you answer, "Jerry and me."

B. When your boss asks, "Who's going to the meeting?" you answer, "Jerry and I."

SUBJECT/OBJECT (2)

A. John is a better writer than me.

B. John is a better writer than I.

NUMBER AGREEMENT

A. Each of the team members are writing their own reports.

B. Each of the team members is writing their own reports.

C. Each of the team members is writing his or her own report.

ADVERBS AND ADJECTIVES

A. We wanted all the designs to look differently.
B. We wanted all the designs to look different.

Answers: B, B, C, B

....

Business Phone Etiquette

Think about how frustrated you become when someone uses a phone inappropriately. Here are some suggestions on how to avoid the most egregious telephone errors at the office:

FACE-TO-FACE VS. PHONE CALL: If you're having a conversation with a person face-to-face, that conversation *should always take precedence over a phone call.* Use the "Do Not Disturb" feature, in which the call is automatically routed to your voice mail, or let your answering machine pick up the call. If you don't have a "Do Not Disturb" feature or an answering device, you may have to answer the phone. In this case, tell the caller that you're busy and will call him back later. One caveat: if you are expecting a call you feel you *must* take, let the person who is with you know the circumstances in advance, and offer to meet with him another time if it would be more convenient.

PLACING SOMEONE ON HOLD: If you put a person on hold, do so for a short period of time—no more than a minute or two, at the most. If there's a problem, get back to him and explain the situation briefly. If you are the one being put on hold and the wait lasts more than three minutes, hang up and call back later. (When you do, try your best not to let your annoyance shine through.)

IDENTIFY YOURSELF: There is nothing more frustrating than getting a call and not knowing whom you're speaking to. Always start your conversation by identifying yourself: "Hi, Tom, this is Jim Smith at Aerospace"—or, if you know Tom somewhat: "Hi, Tom, this is Jim Smith"—or, if Tom is a good friend: "Hi, Tom, Jim here. How about lunch today?" If someone calls you and doesn't identify himself, take the first opportunity to say, "Thank you for calling, but I want to be sure whom I'm speaking to. You are—?"

MAKE YOUR CALLS YOURSELF: I know I'll catch flack for this, but I bristle whenever I get a call that starts, "Hello, Mr. Post, this is Thomas, Mr. Jones's assistant at Aerospace. Mr. Jones would like to speak with you. Can you hold a minute while I get him on the line?" There's something fundamentally wrong with this picture. Mr. Jones is calling *me,* and now he's putting *me* on hold to wait for *him.* Hey, Mr. Jones, my time is valuable, too. Have the courtesy to make the call yourself, and start the conversation on the right foot.

ANSWERING CALLS: "Hi, this is Acme Widget Company, maker of the best widgets in the world. This is Bruce. May I help you?"

TRY ANSWERING THE PHONE: If a phone is ringing, don't always wait for someone else to answer it. "Hi, this is Bill Jones at Aerospace. Can I help you?" Mr. Jones just went up ten notches in my estimation. Here he is, the head cheese, and he's answering the phone. I know one CEO who takes a regular turn answering calls at his company's call center. Imagine the shock when a person calls with a question or complaint and hears the company's CEO on the other end of the line. And imagine the attitude of the people who work at the call center, seeing their CEO sharing in their frustrations and experiencing firsthand the issues they have to deal with.

TAKE EFFICIENT MESSAGES: When you take a message for a colleague, write down your name, the date and time of the call, the caller's name, company, and phone number, and a brief reason for the call. Finally, indicate whether your colleague should return the call, or if the caller will call back later.

SPEAKERPHONES: Any time you are going to use the speakerphone feature, let the person on the other end of the line know right away that he or she is on a speakerphone, and then immediately introduce anyone else who is in the room with you. Have each person say "Hello" in a clear voice as you introduce them, so that the caller can identify the voices of the different participants.

CALL WAITING: Maybe you work at home or in a small office with call waiting, rather than multiple phone lines. When you hear that call-waiting beep, ask the person you're talking to if he or she can hold for just

Telephone Basics

Even though the person on the other end of the line can't see you (at least not yet), she or he *can* hear you. If you're not careful, the things you do or the sounds you make can range from annoying to downright gross. When you're talking on the phone . . .

Don't multi-task: Sounds like typing on a keyboard or shuffling papers can easily be overheard. They indicate one thing to the caller: your attention is elsewhere.

Don't chew gum or eat while you're on the phone: Enough said.

Turn off radios, stereos, and other sound devices: They can drown out your voice and make conversation difficult.

Don't sneeze or cough or blow your nose into the receiver: The other person may be shocked by the freight train coming through their phone. Besides, think of all the germs you just left on the phone for the next person to catch.

Set the receiver down gently: Loud banging noises tend to be amplified on the receiving end.

Don't engage in subterfuges: Never arrange for another person to listen in on a conversation unannounced—even a secretary or assistant. And never record a call without letting the other person know it is being recorded.

Don't try to talk to someone who is on the phone with someone else: This is one of my pet peeves. I don't multi-task well—so when I'm on a call, and an associate pops into my office and starts showing me something or tries to mouth a message, I wave them away. I can't carry on two conversations at once, and I suggest that you don't ask your co-workers to do it, either. Come back when your colleague's call is completed.

a brief moment. Talk to the new caller only long enough to tell him or her that you'll have to call back, then return to the first person and complete your conversation. When your call is done, then—and only then—call the second caller back.

Voice Mail

Do the person you are calling—and yourself—a favor: *leave coherent messages.* "Hi, this is Bill Jones at Aerospace. Tom, I'm sorry I missed you. Could you call me back at 555-1212? I'm calling to discuss . . ."

Keep the description of why you are calling short—two or three sentences at most. Always start your message by stating your name, company, and the number you can be reached at. At the conclusion of the message, repeat your phone number—slowly and clearly. I hate it when a person leaves me a rambling message, tacking on the number only at the bitter end, and then says the number in such a garbled or rushed way that I have to listen to the whole message a second time to get it right.

I met a woman once at a seminar who told me she has a hard time leaving voice mail recordings, because she gets tongue-tied. Her solution is to write out her message *before* she makes the call. If she's faced with voice mail, she simply reads her message. Result: she always projects a professional image that reflects positively on her.

The Cell Phone

Cell phones are one of the most useful *and* one of the most misused tools in business today. The reason is simple: too many people have become slaves to their cell phones. Their thinking goes something like this: "I've got a cell phone now, so I've got to have it on all the time because now I can be reached any time, any place—and I'm so important that people need to be able to reach me any time, any place." One wonders how we ever survived without cell phones. The answer is: we survived just fine.

Master your cell phone: turn it off.

That's the long and the short of it. Use your cell phone when you need to use it, of course. But leave it on only when you know that you can answer it without disturbing other people. If you do use your cell phone for business in a public place, remember that even though you may not know the other people around you, that *doesn't* mean your conversation isn't disturbing them. Either move to a more private place, or don't make or take the call. It's *not* other people's job to move away from

Etiquette Imperative

....

Turn your cell phone off whenever you are in a situation where it will disturb the people around you.

....

Cell Phone Anarchy

A word to the wise: *cell phone conversations aren't private.* When you're sitting on a commuter train and your phone rings and it's a colleague who wants to talk with you about the fine points of your latest contract negotiations, do everyone on the train a favor—*stop the conversation,* then and there. The same holds true when you're on a subway and you answer your phone and your colleague wants to hear all about your hot date from the night before. Trust me: the people around you don't want to hear the details, so do everyone on the subway a favor—*stop the conversation,* then and there.

your conversation—it's your job to move your conversation away from them.

E-mails

I wish I had a dollar for every inappropriate e-mail that has ever been sent. If I did, I'd be a very rich man.

E-mail is a great communication tool. Here are three rules that will make it even greater.

RULE #1: If you can't post it on a bulletin board for anyone to read, then don't send it. I have heard dozens of stories about chagrined e-mail senders who discovered that what they thought was a private communication had become a very public embarrassment—in some cases resulting in lost jobs. Every e-mail is a public document.

RULE #2: Use the "draft" or "send later" feature on your e-mail. Proofread and reread every one of your cyber-communications before you send it—because once it's gone, it's out there.

RULE #3: Make it easy to read. I recommend using fonts that have serifs—those little extra marks on the ends of some letters. They help the reader to scan the line. Also, avoid using ALL CAPITALS in your e-mails. They indicate yelling (projecting anger) and are also difficult to read.

Letters and Memos

Finally, we come to letters and memos: real, physical communications processed on paper (they used to be typed—now they're typically printed from a computer) or sometimes even handwritten with a pen.

Here's the weird truth about this age of e-mail: these days, real letters—"snail mail," delivered through the postal service or by an overnight carrier or hand-carried by a personal courier—have become *the* means of communicating when you want to say, "This is really important," or "This is really personal," or when you want to thank someone in the most respectful way possible. Snail mail stands out.

The Stationery Drawer

For your snail mail communications, keep a stationery drawer stocked with the following items.

Business stationery: 8½ × 11-inch sheets of high-quality paper, printed with your company name and logo. Local quick printers can help you find the right stock. Take the time to look at the color and tone variations and to feel the paper with your hands. Ask yourself: "Is it substantial enough, while still being subtle enough to convey my image?"

Business envelopes: Choose a standard #10 envelope that holds a sheet of stationery folded in thirds. The paper stock should match the business stationery stock, with your business name and address printed in the return address corner of the envelope.

Monarch sheets: These are smaller 7¼ × 10½-inch sheets made of the same paper stock as your business stationery. Monarch sheets are for personal notes. They should have your name and address printed on them, but no business logo. They come with matching envelopes.

Correspondence cards: Usually made of a heavyweight paper, correspondence cards are used to write brief notes by hand. The typical size for a correspondence card is 4¼ × 6½ inches. Matching envelopes are usually ordered at the same time.

Folded notes and informals: These are small, folded-over sheets on which you handwrite your message. They are great for brief personal messages.

24

....

Everyday Business
Manners

A S WE SAW IN chapter 22, the way you handle yourself matters in
business: if you exhibit demeaning behavior or a superior attitude,
this can and will have a powerfully negative effect on the way your colleagues view you. When it comes to everyday manners, the impact is
more subtle—but here, too, the judgments that others make about you
can mean the difference between your success or failure.

For example, in today's gender-neutral business environment, men
are not supposed to treat a woman any differently than they would
another man. Personally, I've never held a chair for a man—and in fact,
proper business etiquette says that a man should *not* hold the chair for a
woman. The problem men face here is that many women—at least many
of those who responded to the Post Survey—still want a man to hold a
chair for them at a work-related social dinner. Suddenly, this "black and
white" rule becomes murky gray.

The key to solving any business etiquette dilemma is to apply the principles of etiquette in a thoughtful way: at a casual business lunch, I would
follow the standard guideline and refrain from holding the chair for a
female colleague. If I'm seated next to a female colleague at an elegant

business dinner, as we approach our chairs I will look over at her and ask, "May I get your chair for you?" Now I've made it *her* choice, and she can respond in whatever way makes her feel most comfortable: "No, thank you, I'm all set"—or, "Why, yes, Peter. Thank you."

Rather than simply holding the chair and risking offending my co-worker, consideration requires me to ask her what her preference is. By asking this question, I varied the guideline in a way that made both of us feel comfortable—and that is what etiquette is all about.

Around the Office

Mr. or Ms.?

When you start a new job, one of the first issues you'll face as a new employee is how you should address your colleagues, especially people in a position senior to your own. At a large company, you'll usually be shown around by a person from your department or from the company's human resources department. During that first-day tour, ask this question right up front: "Excuse me—but I was wondering how I should address the vice president of marketing. Is it Ms. Smith, or Jane?" Remember, everybody there had a first day once.

Watch, listen, and learn. Be an observer of human nature—then emu-

---

Workplace Cultures

Every workplace is a unique culture, with its own customs, rules, and conventions. One of the most important things you can do when you're starting a new job is to learn as much as you can about your new work culture. In one company, for example, everyone may call everyone else by their first names—while in another corporate culture, you might be expected to address the senior managers as "Mr." or "Ms."

If you deal with clients or suppliers as part of your job, you also need to learn about *their* cultures. Here in Vermont, I might choose to dress one way if I'm asked to attend a meeting at Ben and Jerry's Ice Cream, and a very different way for a meeting at a local bank. In both cases, I'm entering another company's culture—and I want to show them that I respect and understand that culture.

Etiquette Imperative

....

Every workplace you enter is a new culture with its own rules.
Your job is to learn these rules and work within them.

Whatever the situation, if you are unsure of what to do, watch the
people around you for clues and follow their lead.

....

late what you see others doing. If everyone else calls your boss Ms. Smith,
the odds are very good that you should do the same. Don't be shy about
asking your co-workers for advice.

Gossip

Wherever men and women gather for work, tongues will wag. People
talk behind other people's backs in every office—so why shouldn't you
get in on the act, too?

Here's why: gossip and talking behind other people's backs creates
hard feelings. Hard feelings and the other distractions stemming from
rude behavior at the workplace lower employee morale. Productivity
takes a hit, and employee retention suffers. Ultimately, all these factors
drive down profits, and if profits go south, you're going to feel it in your
pocketbook—or worse.

So make a pact with yourself: don't gossip.

If you see others gossiping, what should you do? At the very least,
refuse to participate, by leaving the conversation at once. Or you can go
one step better, by letting the group know how you feel: "Hey, let's back
off. Please." Then change the subject: "Anyway, I'm more interested in
whether anyone saw the Giants blow that twenty-four-point lead in last
night's playoff game. Can you believe they did that?"

Cubicle Etiquette

Cubicles are here to stay. As an efficient way for businesses to maxi-
mize the value of office space, they're unbeatable. But while a cubicle
offers a modicum of privacy, it's not the same as having an office with a
door that you can shut. The problems that occur in cubicles usually have
to do with this lack of a truly private space. These include:

NOISE. The background hum in an open office is bad enough. When you add loud conversations (either in person or over the phone), you have a recipe for real frustration. *Noise interferes with a person's ability to work.* While you can't do much about the normal background noise in your area, you *can* work to keep down the noise you generate, by lowering your voice and using headphones to listen to music.

CONVERSATIONS. A short Q & A session with a colleague is fine—but a longer consultation or a group discussion should be taken to a conference room, an available private office, or the break room. If private space is not available, you and your visitor(s) will need to learn to talk quietly.

PHONE VOICE. Make a conscious effort to lower your voice. Men, in particular, tend to talk louder than normal when they get on a phone.

PERSONAL PHONE CALLS. Your company may have a policy about no personal calls on the job. If so, follow it. If there is no stated policy, you should still be careful not to abuse your phone privileges.

BURPS, SLURPS, SMACKS. Smacking gum, burping, slurping coffee— these noises travel and are disgusting to others. A quick nose blow is okay, but if you have to clear your sinuses and need to go at it with gusto, take a bathroom break and go at it there.

PRAIRIE-DOGGING. The neat thing about cubicles is how easy they make it for a person to pop his head above the cubicle wall and interject himself into a conversation in the next cubicle. Don't prairie-dog. Instead, walk around and enter the other cubicle through the entrance, as you would do in an office. Prairie-dogging is a telltale sign that you've been eavesdropping. I realize it can be hard to intentionally *not* hear a conversation in the next cubicle—but it's your responsibility to show respect for other people's privacy by not jumping up and *admitting* to them that you've been listening in.

Gifts

An assistant producer at a talk show once asked me, "Peter, I'm pretty new here, and recently it was the senior producer's birthday. I decided to give her a nice bottle of wine as a birthday gift. Was this appropriate?"

"No," I answered. "Here's why: when workers start individually giving gifts to a manager, competition and one-upsmanship are right around the corner. Let's say your bottle of wine cost twenty-five dollars. As your co-worker, I'm now wondering—are you being a brownnoser? Does this mean everyone else has to match it? Maybe I don't have twenty-five dollars. Are you trying to make me look bad?"

The only appropriate way for employees to give a gift to a manager is as a group. Otherwise, acknowledge the birthday on the day in question by saying, "Happy Birthday."

Holiday gift-giving is another source of workplace angst. Should you buy a gift for everyone in your office? Answer: no. Offices usually have a tradition of some kind about holiday gifts, such as the Secret Santa, with gift values held to a small dollar amount.

It's fine to go ahead and give a gift to one or two people you're especially close to, but do the gift-giving in private, out of the sight and hearing of other employees. Remember, your goal is to show your appreciation to a specific person.

Finally, just because you give someone a gift, *don't* expect one in return.

Kitchen and Food

We have had three kitchen wars at my advertising agency. Each one was over a different issue, and each one almost resulted in the kitchen being shut down for good.

The first war involved a food-theft problem. Someone's delicious leftovers disappeared one day, and that person was *not* happy. The guideline here is really simple: what's yours is yours—and what's not yours, you leave alone.

The second war was over the refrigerator. Some food containers had been left in there so long that they'd started taking on a life of their own. Solution: we asked everyone to be vigilant about removing any old lunches or snacks. Everyone's gotten better about this, and we still have a refrigerator.

The third war was over people leaving dirty plates and glasses in the sink. It boggles my imagination as to how this could even be a problem. Where's the ambiguity here? You use a plate or a glass, you bring it to the sink, you wash it, you dry it, and you put it away.

The Water Cooler

A quick work break is a great thing. It's an opportunity to stretch your legs, shake out the cobwebs, and recharge yourself. But there are some problems that can arise, especially if you have a couple of co-workers who are in the habit of taking a break at the same time you do.

BREAKING TOO OFTEN: Taking a break once in the morning and once in the afternoon makes sense. Taking a break every fifteen minutes, however, will quickly mark you as a shirker.

BREAKING TOO LONG: Be careful—a ten-minute break can suddenly grow into a half-hour break. Then, before you know it, tongues are wagging and managers are scowling.

INAPPROPRIATE CONVERSATION: An increasing number of companies now have rules outlining appropriate and inappropriate topics for office conversation. Jokes may be acceptable in one company and taboo in another. Gossiping is never acceptable. The same goes for "trash talking" the company and/or its policies. Instead, focus on "safe" subjects such as movies, sports, entertainment, music. And if the conversation veers where it shouldn't, excuse yourself and head back to work.

Hygiene

People who don't wash often enough, or who don't use a deodorant and consequently smell unpleasant, are hurting their opportunity to have good relationships with colleagues and negatively impacting their chances for promotion. The easiest way to deal with the problem is to wash regularly—once a day—and use a deodorant, preferably one with little or no scent. Fresh clothes each day are another must. At the very least, give your shirt or other clothes the "sniff" test—and be honest with yourself about the results.

The other big problem area involves scents—cologne, perfume, or scented deodorants. Splashing on the cologne or perfume might make heads turn when you walk by—but maybe for the wrong reason. In fact, many organizations now have "no-scent" policies.

Etiquette Imperative

....

If people focus on your clothes rather than on you, then you've chosen the wrong clothes to wear.

....

In either case, you don't want people sitting as far away from you as possible because of your smell. This is *not* good for building positive relationships.

Why Follow Company Policy?

....

Why do you have to follow your company's policies? Because it's their business, and they set the rules. If you don't like the rules, then that company may not be the right place for you. One thing you can be sure of, though, is that if you buck the rules, your employers will not be pleased with you.

....

Clothing

Clothing is a difficult issue. What you consider to be "casually appropriate," your boss may consider to be inappropriate. When you're dressing for work, keep this point in mind: if there's a company dress policy and your clothes breach that policy, then people will focus on your clothes, and not on you.

If you wear a pair of jeans and a collarless shirt to the office and everyone else is wearing a coat and tie, your clothes will make you stand out. If you wear a three-piece suit to an interview, on the other hand, and the people interviewing you are all wearing polo shirts and khakis, then they will focus on your clothes, and not on you.

To help you dress for success, including the tricky distinction between "business casual" and "business professional" attire, here are some guidelines:

Men—Professional

ACCEPTABLE

Suits—three-piece, two-piece, two-buttoned or three-buttoned, wool or cotton

Blazers or sports jacket with tie

Slacks

Dress shirts or Oxford button-down

Vest

Overcoats or raincoat

Oxfords, wingtips, or loafers

Dark socks

NOT ACCEPTABLE

Loud colors or bold patterns

Wearing spread collar without a tie

Athletic shoes

White socks

Fur coats

Showy belt buckles

Men—Casual

ACCEPTABLE

Blazers

Shirts—Oxford style button-down collars

Turtleneck shirts

Shortsleeved knit shirts

Khaki slacks

V-neck or crewneck sweaters

Informal ties

NOT ACCEPTABLE

T-shirts with slogans, sayings, or cartoons

Torn or wornout jeans

Anything shiny or too tight

Sandals

Tank tops

Shorts

Does Business Casual Mean That I Can Wear Jeans and a T-shirt?

The issue of whether jeans are allowed or not is determined by the policy of each individual workplace. In some places jeans are fine, and others they are not. It is *never* acceptable, however, to wear jeans that are torn, have holes in them, are stained, are too tight, and/or are very worn out. This applies to both men and women.

The same guidelines apply to T-shirts: in some companies, for example, wearing the company T-shirt with a logo is perfectly acceptable, but that's all. If T-shirts are allowed at your office, your shirts should always be clean, in good condition, and slogan free.

25

Business Social Events

I T'S THREE O'CLOCK IN the afternoon, just another ordinary working day, when suddenly the phone rings. It's your company's sales manager at the other end of the line: "Tom, I just got off the phone with Bill Jones at Aerospace. They signed the contract today. I'm hosting a dinner tomorrow night to celebrate. You worked hard on the details, so I was hoping you might join us."

Your sales manager is right: you *did* work hard, and celebrating the victory with the client will be a real honor. Congratulations!

Now . . . be careful.

The dinner with client and colleagues is a business function, not a social function—even if it is a "celebration." No matter how relaxed the atmosphere is, and no matter how friendly and collegial everybody feels, how you conduct yourself at the dinner *will* reflect on you the next day and in the future.

This holds true for every business social event you will ever take part in—not to mention many events that don't even appear to be business-related.

Business social events offer an opportunity to combine pleasure with work, particularly the relationship-building aspect of work—and that's exactly the part that can either bolster your success or hurt it. Whether you're shmoozing at a business social hour, attending a sit-down dinner, or going on a business-related outing, etiquette can make all the difference in how well you connect with other people. Here's how.

The Business Social Mixer

There are several versions of the business social mixer: it could be an internal office cocktail event, or a company-sponsored event for clients and prospects, or an event hosted by a client, or an association event (such as a local chamber of commerce mixer) at which you're representing your company, or an event that's held as part of a conference or seminar.

Whatever the nature of the gathering, the key point to keep in mind is that your company *hasn't* asked you to attend simply to eat, drink, and have a good time. At all of these events—with the possible exception of the internal company gathering—you will be expected to mix and mingle, and to meet new people and develop new contacts while also building on your existing relationships.

Introductions

Before you walk in the door at one of these events, you need to know how to introduce yourself and others correctly. Introductions are the first moment of interaction, and they form the basis of people's first impressions. It's *imperative* that you get the introduction right. When you do, each participant will feel comfortable and ready to move on to getting to know the other person better. When you blow an introduction, the focus shifts to the mistake, and the opportunity to ignite a new relationship is lost.

Check the tips on meeting and greeting in chapter 7. Remember, the four steps when introducing yourself are:

> Stand up

> Look the other person in the eyes and smile

> Say your name clearly

> Offer a firm handshake

If you are in a position to introduce two people, speak to the more important person first. "Mr. Client, I'd like to introduce Mr. Bryant to you. Mr. Bryant is our new senior vice president of sales."

Alcohol

At all business social events, the biggest single source of trouble is alcohol. If you are even slightly inebriated, you won't be able to concentrate fully on your real task of fostering new relationships and enhancing existing ones.

If you want to have an alcoholic beverage, nurse it slowly and make it last. Or you can make things even easier on yourself by forgoing alcohol completely. In today's business world, it's perfectly respectable not to imbibe at all. Soda water, soda, or juice are totally acceptable alternatives.

Conversing

Many people are petrified at the idea of starting a conversation with a stranger at a business social function. Fortunately, you can get over this fear. Here are two tricks that will really help:

1. **Practice, practice, practice.** Get into the habit of talking to "safe strangers" whenever you encounter them, including taxi-cab drivers, sales clerks, checkout counter people, the FedEx delivery person, and so on.

2. **Keep up to date on a variety of topics.** Sports, politics, entertainment, music, popular books, movies, business news, and travel are all topics that most people have at least some interest in and enjoy talking about. I read the paper every day—including the national and local news, the sports, even the comics. I keep up on the entertainment news and gossip, and I make a point of channel-surfing and developing some opinions as to which TV shows I really like. *Now* I've got topics to talk about!

Working the Room

The business social event is a terrific opportunity to land new business, solidify existing relationships, and discover new candidates for future prospecting. The craft of "working the room"—making your way steadily and purposefully from person to person—provides you with a chance to meet and interact with lots of people. Not only is this skill helpful to you in broadening your network, but as you master the art of being a good conversationalist, other people will recognize your talent and be impressed by it.

The following tips will help you work any room effectively:

Before you go to the event . . .

SET GOALS FOR YOURSELF. By that, I *don't* mean how many shrimp you can eat. Develop a list of people you want to meet, and a plan of action for meeting them.

RESEARCH. Once you've developed this list, find out more about the people you hope to meet. Learn about their background and their non-business interests—then record this information in your contact management system, so you have it at your fingertips for future use.

When you're at the event . . .

STAND UP AND WALK AROUND THE ROOM. Don't sit in one place, or stand in one corner the entire time.

MOVE OUT OF YOUR COMFORT ZONE. Challenge yourself: don't stand there safely talking shop with your co-workers all evening long. Instead, consciously choose to approach people you don't know, introduce yourself, and strike up a conversation. When you are in a conversation, make sure you include all the other people in the group. The more you do this, the easier it will get.

WATCH FOR CLUES AS YOU APPROACH PEOPLE. Observe their body language for signs of receptivity. Listen to how they welcome you (or don't) into their conversation. Not everybody will be receptive to your approach. If someone blows you off, move on to someone else.

OPEN CONVERSATIONS ON AN UPBEAT NOTE. Always start with a positive comment or question. Don't be negative, either in tone or substance. Use open-ended questions to promote dialogue.

LOOK FOR TOPICS OF COMMON INTEREST. If you are at a person's house for a business dinner, look around for clues to their interests in photos, objects, and books.

SEEK OUT NEW AND DIFFERENT PEOPLE. Relish the opportunity to bridge generational and cultural gaps.

CONNECT AND THEN MOVE ON. After a few minutes of conversation, gently excuse yourself from the group you're with and move on to another person or group.

Remember, since you're representing your company, the way you handle yourself will reflect on you *and* on your employer. Don't be surprised if word gets back to others in your company about how you conducted yourself—be it good or bad.

The Business Meal

The business meal is a great opportunity to cement a relationship. It's also a great opportunity to ruin one. There are no job skills to fall back

---

Breaking Up a Monopoly

Despite your best efforts, every now and then at a business social event you'll find yourself cornered by someone who latches on and won't let go. You know your mission is to mix and mingle—so how do you extricate yourself from a conversation with a monopolizer without being rude or dishonest?

➤ Saying that you've got to go to the bathroom and then simply walking over to the bar or joining another group is poor etiquette. If you excuse yourself by saying you need to go to the bathroom, then by all means go and make your visit there. You're then free to return and join a new group.

➤ A better option is simply to be firm and disengage—but do it tactfully: "Jerry, it's been a pleasure catching up with you—but my boss laid it on the line with me today. I need to work the room and make some new contacts tonight. So, if you'll excuse me, I see one of the people I'm supposed to talk with. Take care." And then walk away.

on: everything rests on how you present yourself, how you interact with the other people at the meal, and how you represent your company.

Don't Be Late

I met Jim at a seminar, and he told me the following story: Jim understands the value of being on time, and of knowing the culture you are in. His friend doesn't. The friend, a salesman, traveled to the Netherlands to do a deal. His European hosts invited him to a luncheon, and he showed up late. Shortly after that, the European hosts informed Jim that his friend would not get the deal. How could they expect him to make good on his promises, they explained to Jim, if he couldn't even show up on time at a restaurant?

If you are hosting the business meal, be sure to be there five to ten minutes early. This will give you a chance to check the table and make sure everything is acceptable, and to figure out where people will sit. If you plan to serve wine, talk with the maître d' or wine steward about an appropriate selection. One especially nice touch is to arrange for payment of the bill ahead of time, so you don't have to deal with a check arriving at the table at the end of the meal. Finally, hit the men's room, do what you need to, then wash your hands, comb your hair, and make sure you are looking sharp. Five minutes early sure beats five minutes late!

If you're a guest at the business meal, don't be late, either. If you are unavoidably delayed for some reason, call the restaurant (of course you were smart enough to write down the phone number before leaving your office, right?), ask them to let your host know that you're running late, and give an estimate of when you think you'll arrive.

Who Pays?

It's simple, really. At a business meal, whoever does the inviting does the paying.

When You're the Host

If you are the host of a business meal, you should:

➢ Arrange for the reservation

➢ Do the inviting

➤ Make sure your cell phone and pager are turned off

➤ Indicate where you would like people to sit, making especially sure to offer the best seat to the most important guest (usually by seating that person to your right)

➤ Help people with the menu selections by suggesting a couple of particularly good items (of course you've been careful to choose a restaurant that you've been to before, so you know what is especially good)

➤ Select wine for the table

➤ Direct the conversation by introducing topics

➤ Watch to make sure that all the guests are engaged and enjoying themselves, and that no one is stuck being a wallflower

➤ Introduce any business discussion *after* the main course has been completed

➤ Pay the bill

➤ Finally, at the end of the meal, indicate when it's time to depart, and thank everyone for coming

When You're the Guest

If you are the guest at a business meal, you should:

➤ Watch for clues from your host as to where he or she wants you to sit

➤ Make sure your cell phone and pager are turned off

➤ Listen to and take part in the conversation, but don't dominate it

➤ Introduce yourself to and converse with the people seated on both your right and your left

➤ Order a moderate, mid-priced meal—unless the host insists that you try the "best filet mignon in the state"

➤ Order a drink *only* if your host and others order drinks as well— and then nurse that drink along slowly. If others at the table *do* choose to order drinks or wine, there is no imperative saying that you have to join in—fruit juice, sparkling water, or soda are all excellent alternatives. (Personally, I don't drink alcohol at business social events. It relieves me of having to make this decision.)

➢ Conduct yourself with the best table manners possible (see chapter 16)—and when you are not sure what to do, watch to see what others are doing, then imitate them. If that doesn't work, then make a choice based on doing whatever you think shows the most consideration for the people around you.

➢ Wait for your host to bring up any business topics. Typically, business talk is engaged in only after the main course is completed. Since the host invited you, it's up to him or her to bring up any business issues.

➢ At the end of the meal, thank your dining partners and your host. Then, when you get home or the first thing next morning at the office, handwrite a thank-you note on a correspondence card that you keep in your stationery drawer (see chapter 23).

Afterword

THROUGHOUT THIS BOOK, I'VE mentioned again and again that situations arise for which there is no specific manners rule. That's when I use the essential principles of etiquette—consideration, respect, and honesty—to figure out what to do.

When I respond to etiquette questions, I use a very definable system to develop answers when traditional manners don't fit the situation. It's a simple five-step process that anyone can use:

1. **START WITH CONSIDERATION.** Be aware of how a current situation *affects* everyone involved.

2. **DEVELOP SOME SPECIFIC SOLUTIONS.** Try to think of all the different ways you could choose to *resolve* the situation.

3. **SHOW RESPECT FOR EACH PERSON INVOLVED.** Examine how each solution affects each person.

4. **BE HONEST WITH YOURSELF.** Review again how your solution resolves the situation for each person. Be truthful with yourself as you select the solution that best solves the problem for *all* the people involved.

5. **ADJUST YOUR SOLUTION AS NECESSARY.** If needed, make any necessary changes, and then review the revised solution to make sure that it is now the best resolution possible.

When you use this process, the outcome for you is the same: confidence. When you feel confident, you exude confidence. When you exude confidence, people react positively to you.

That is why etiquette is valuable to you. Use it, enjoy how people respond to you, and watch yourself become ever more successful in your daily life, your social life, and your work life. Good luck!

INDEX

....

EMILY POST 1873 TO 1960

....

Emily Post began her career as a writer at the age of thirty-one. Her romantic stories of European and American society were serialized in *Vanity Fair, Collier's, McCall's,* and other popular magazines. Many were also successfully published in book form.

Upon its publication in 1922, her book, *Etiquette,* topped the nonfiction bestseller list, and the phrase "according to Emily Post" soon entered our language as the last word on the subject of social conduct. Mrs. Post, who as a girl had been told that well-bred women should not work, was suddenly a pioneering American woman. Her numerous books, a syndicated newspaper column, and a regular network radio program made Emily Post a figure of national stature and importance throughout the rest of her life.

"Good manners reflect something from inside—an innate sense of consideration for others and respect for self."

—Emily Post